Judith Dimond began writing – both  retiring from a career in equality and many years in the Citizens Advice S Martin's and St Paul's Church in Canterbury, she is also a Companion of the Society of St Francis, and leads occasional workshops on poetry and prayer. She lives with her husband in what was once a pub, and together they enjoy exploring the coasts of Kent and northern France. She is also the author of *Gazing on the Gospels, Years A, B and C* (SPCK, 2008, 2009, 2010).

FRIENDS, FOES AND FAMILIES

Lenten meditations on Bible characters and relationships

Judith Dimond

First published in Great Britain in 2012

Society for Promoting Christian Knowledge
36 Causton Street
London SW1P 4ST
www.spckpublishing.co.uk

British Library Cataloguing-in-Publication Data
A catalogue record for this book is available from the British Library

ISBN 978–0–281–06456–4
eBook ISBN 978–0–281–06958–3

Typeset by Graphicraft Limited, Hong Kong
Manufacture managed by Jellyfish
First printed in Great Britain by CPI Group
Subsequently digitally printed in Great Britain

Produced on paper from sustainable forests

To my family

Thanks, as ever, to Paul,
my friend and mentor, and also
to everyone at SPCK

What therefore we need is not a stronger will,
but a deeper insight,
not more strength, but more light.

(H. A. Williams, *True Wilderness*, p. 58)

Contents

Contents

Introduction

Who endowed the heart with wisdom, or gave understanding
to the mind?   (Job 38.36, NIV 1984)

This is a book about relationships, particularly as recounted in the Scriptures. Using both Old and New Testament characters, some less well remembered than others, we will challenge ourselves to find, in the lives of people who lived long ago, reflections of our own relationships in all their fragility. Through these often larger than life stories, our own predicaments may be revealed in a clearer light, and we may be surprised into fresh ways of understanding. It is a truism that we learn more from our failures than our successes, so I make no apology for the emphasis in the book on the dysfunctional. Through the lives of some of the characters who fill the pages of our Scriptures, we see the common pattern of wilderness, death and resurrection repeated over and over again, and each daily reflection studies one or other of this threefold pattern.

Perhaps we will see ourselves in one of the characters, or our choices in their own decisions, our failures in their mistakes, and loving solutions in their successes. For the Bible is the 'culminating ideal of morality and spirituality', as Keith Ward explained in his marvellous retelling of the Pentateuch (*The Promise*, p. ix). Though our decisions always have implications for others as well as ourselves, we often treat a decision as ours and ours alone, ignoring God's involvement altogether.

Each story will be approached according to the values of the final episode – the cross and resurrection of Jesus. That is why there is space for prayer within each piece. If we live within relationships, we are forced to make choices, so we had better pray for 'a discerning heart' (1 Kings 3.9). Like Solomon, whose prayer this was, we must never cease praying for wisdom, so that when we find ourselves at a pivotal moment in our lives, we are clear-sighted, not confused, capable and not frozen in indecision. We must start with a deliberate intention to search for wisdom; it will not drop from the sky as God's gift of manna did, but comes only to those alert and aware that the hard work of attention is required of them.

Where is wisdom to be found? Why do some people seem to have it inbuilt, others have to learn it through trial and tribulation, and others never find it? Some people spend all their lives knowing something at an intellectual level, but never reaching the point that allows compassion to penetrate. Some never reach enlightenment about the world outside themselves, because they never achieve self-knowledge of what is hidden deep within. Because we need help in this, the wisest decisions are those we make which integrate our minds and our hearts with Christ's teaching and example.

* * *

This book traces a line from initial confusion and repeated crises to disaster and beyond disaster to the possibility of transformed lives. This is the same trajectory we follow all our lives, in all our relationships. It is also the basic shape of our Bible – from the confusion and failures of the Old Testament, haltingly discerning God's universal truths, to the tragedy of the Passion and the renewal of the Resurrection. Our progress is not linear. The Old Testament has flashes of reconciliation, and the New Testament has instances of folly. We still carry outmoded ideas, like redundant vestiges of evolution; like a grumbling appendix, they can still cause an awful lot of pain. One of the pleasures of writing this book has been making connections between the two halves of our Scripture. We meet the alienation of Cain, and of Judas; celebrate the loyalty of Jonathan, and Peter's reconciliation with Jesus. We travel from the blindness of Isaac through the stumblings of numerous women and men labouring in the shadow of selfishness and sin, until we reach the explosion of light which gave Paul new sight. Despite all our mishandlings, God keeps his promise to repair and regenerate.

> I keep asking that the God of our Lord Jesus Christ, the glorious Father, may give you the spirit of wisdom and revelation, so that you may know him better. I pray that the eyes of your heart may be enlightened in order that you may know the hope to which he has called you. (Ephesians 1.17–18)

ASH WEDNESDAY AND INTRODUCTORY WEEK

———•◦•———

But my people would not listen to me . . .
So I gave them over to their stubborn hearts
to follow their own devices.

(Psalm 81.11, 12)

,

Ash Wednesday: in order to know what is in your heart

Mark 1.12, 13

Remember how the LORD your God led you
all the way in the wilderness these forty years,
to humble and test you
in order to know what was in your heart.

(Deuteronomy 8.2)

Deserts are dry, brittle places. No water flows in them and only the occasional dew allows the minimum of life. Dry sand blows in the eyes and coats the lips. Plants wither and leaves shrivel. All around Jesus' feet were the parched skeletons of small creatures who had lost their search for water. Yet the Spirit had banished Jesus here, leaving him no choice in the matter. Sometimes wisdom lies in realizing we are not in control, in not resisting, but allowing a crisis to take us beyond what we thought possible or bearable.

Let the white of these pages which surround the prayers
become a space
for our penitence for the past, our present resolve,
and our future hopes.

In this heat and this thirst, Jesus craved water above anything else. By day he saw a recurring mirage of a verdant oasis, overhung by shady palms, where camels lapped at the water, children paddled and women drew water for the pot. By night he dreamed of his baptism in the Jordan – the cool of the river over his limbs, the drenching of his robes, the shock when water covered his head and trickled over his face, washing away the grit and dust. This was lifesaving water in every sense.

Being cleansed is not as easy as standing under a modern shower or turning on a washing machine. Some of you reading this may remember mothers or grandmothers beating clothes on the scrubbing board, pounding the stains against the wood to release the dirt from the fibres.

> Wash me, and I shall be whiter than snow.
> (Psalm 51.7)

The time Jesus spent in the desert was hard and bitter and parts of our lives will be too. We must not be afraid to shed tears, for they reveal our vulnerability. We fight to hold back our tears because we fear exposing our 'weakness'. But what else is this weakness but an admission that we are suffering, or are open to the suffering of others, or appalled at the injustices of this world? Tears witness to our sorrows, and our sorrows are an acknowledgement that all is not right either within ourselves or the community we inhabit. This flow of tears is proof that our hearts have been touched and these are the times we are most open to the possibility of change.

> Welcome the waiting and the arriving,
> the emptying as well as the fulfilling;
> the struggle as much as the achievement,
> the losing and the gaining;
> welcome the end as well as the beginning,
> for in both are we re-created.

The desert changed Jesus for good. On his return, his mission was to assuage the thirst of all whom he met. It was as if he had vowed never to be thirsty again, and he had learnt the absolute value of water. In John's Gospel, the first miracle he performed on returning from the wilderness was to attend a wedding at Cana and change water into wine. He was making up for all the thirst and hunger of the past forty days and saying: I will not allow this thirst and scarcity to afflict my people, that is not my Father's way. So he went about promising 'a spring of water welling up to eternal life' (John 4.14). This was the stream he'd longed for in the desert.

Jesus planned for us a garden bursting with new life, another paradise, cultivated by the streams of baptism and the tears of his suffering.

Picture this garden like one of the gardens of an Arabian palace. From courtyard to courtyard water flows unceasingly; from one level to another it cascades, always channelled on to the next shady spot. And at its heart stands a fountain, gushing with a superabundant waterfall of grace.

> Restore our fortunes, LORD, like streams in the Negev.
> Those who sow with tears will reap with songs of joy.
>
> (Psalm 126.4, 5)

But Jonah ran away from the Lord

Jonah

> When I run away, rescue me,
> when I argue, answer,
> when I despair, have patience with me,
> when I am foolish, help me to reflect,
> when I am hasty, remind me to pray.

The book of Jonah is a beautifully crafted book of wisdom, disguised as a comic fable, and it is a book about salvation pretending to be a children's bedtime story. When God says to Jonah – Go! we plunge into a plot of escapes and returns, descending and ascending, and lots of argument. By the third verse, Jonah has run away, refusing to carry out God's order to preach repentance to Nineveh. He headed in the opposite direction to God's will and so heaped calamity on his head, and the heads of the innocent sailors whose ship he sailed in. He acted with all the impetuosity of a foolish person, and then tried to ease his conscience with a foolhardy display of heroics, by offering to be thrown overboard. 'It is my fault that this great storm has come upon you,' he declared with a flash of insight.

> This Lent, make me aware of my faults and my folly,
> and make me ready, willing and able to confess.

Jonah rushed about but never reflected, he seemed unable to live the faith he declared so boldly. The sailors did not know this God, but they behaved with more sense and humanity than Jonah, trying to avoid his sacrifice. Though outsiders to the faith, they gain the reader's admiration.

Jonah's descent was complete when he was engulfed by waves and entangled in weeds, and on the point of drowning. He banished himself to a watery wilderness, until along came the unnamed fish.

Surely this would be the end of Jonah? But instead of being execu-
tioner, it was his saviour, not his nemesis but his rescuer. Jonah had
to hit rock bottom before he could come to his senses and begin to
pray from within the fish. This is the pivot of the whole book. Trapped
in the pitch-black of a huge fish belly, in the darkness of the ocean
floor which the sun's rays would never reach, Jonah saw a glimmer
of God's light and began his faltering ascent to wisdom.

This Lent, let us pray using Jonah's words:

> I sank down . . . but you . . . brought my life up from the pit.
> When my life was ebbing away, I remembered you, Lord.
>
> (Jonah 2.6, 7)

A second time God's word was heard by Jonah – Go! Though Jonah
had learnt enough to be obedient, he had learnt neither wisdom nor
compassion. Jonah was furious that the task he'd been set was to save
a heathen city – Nineveh – from its sins. His impulse was a destructive
judgement and a lack of love for a people outside of his community.
Though he was God's servant and prophet, he didn't share God's love
for all of creation. It was Jonah who had the greatest lesson to learn,
not Nineveh. Jonah was already sliding away from discernment, but
Nineveh did learn wisdom, and repented.

> This Lent, I will lift my eyes from myself
> and pay attention to your wilderness world
> where human failure has brought such pain
> and people cry out for healing, homes, food and peace.

Jonah was by then so angry that he lost his temper with God, along
with all sense of proportion. 'It is better for me to die than to live'
(Jonah 4.3). Though he had just declaimed the great recurring credal
statement of the Old Testament, he was only paying lip service to it;
the meaning was not in his heart: 'You are a gracious and compassionate God, slow to anger and abounding in love, a God who relents
from sending calamity' (Jonah 4.2).

The children's story more or less ends with the rescue of Nineveh.
But we adults must read on. Jonah built himself a shelter – a second
version of the hospitable fish – in which to hide and sulk. And God
decided to teach him wisdom not with words but by deeds. He

blessed Jonah's shelter with a cool spreading vine, but just as Jonah got comfortable, he destroyed it. 'I'm angry enough to die,' Jonah peevishly declared, taking God's behaviour as spite. And still God kept calm, and explained with a question – why weep for the loss of this small plant, but not for my people? Why would I ever want to create, in order to destroy?

Jonah's saving grace was that he was always honest and transparent as a little child. But the book ends before we discover if he ever grew up.

> God, you give shade when we are scorched
> and rescue us when we are adrift;
> help me to mature in my faith and grow in wisdom
> through every incident of my life.
> Amen.

Lot lived among the cities of the plain

Genesis 12—14, 18, 19

> When I'm tempted to live on the plain,
> to choose a life of ease and comfort,
> help me think again.

The gruesome story of the destruction of Sodom and Gomorrah is, in fact, the dramatic peak of the story of Lot, Abraham's nephew, and his life is a sub-plot of Abraham's saga. If Abraham was renowned for his faith and trust, what was Lot's dominant characteristic? Surely it was a foolishness made obvious through laziness and vacillation. Lot teaches us the danger of too much hesitation.

Already in Abraham's shadow when the extended family left Ur for Haran, Lot continued with Abraham on to Canaan. Together they thrived until their combined herds put such a strain on the local economy that Abraham decided they must part. Abraham graciously gave Lot the choice of where to settle, and Lot settled for the easy option.

There he lived 'among the cities of the plain and pitched his tents near Sodom' (Genesis 13.12), where he soon succumbed to temptation and moved into town. When warfare overtook the plain, the town was ransacked and Lot, his family and possessions, were carried off. So far we might excuse Lot for just having bad luck, but it was Uncle Abraham who had to come to his rescue.

> Holy God, I live close to the bright lights
> where I compromise my ideals and my honour.
> Preserve me from corruption.

We next meet Lot as a player in Abraham's great encounter with God, who comes disguised as three visitors (Chapter 18). After God had confided his plan to obliterate the cities, Abraham remained standing before the Lord, as he debated, 'Will you sweep away the righteous with the wicked?' So the three visitors descended to Sodom to warn the righteous, and met Lot sitting by the gateway. His easy-going nature and laissez-faire attitudes had got him into very bad company. Lot gave hospitality to the Visitors, but the depraved men of Sodom attacked. Anxious to protect his guests, Lot offered to sacrifice his virgin daughters: 'and you can do what you like with them'. We'll see some very poor attitudes towards women during our exploration of Genesis, but none more flagrant than this!

All Lot's cosying up to the locals was of no avail. 'This fellow came here as a foreigner and now he wants to play the judge!' they taunted. So, keeping his head down didn't turn out to be a successful strategy.

> Forgive me the sins I slip into through association,
> my values tarnished and my resolve weakened.
> Help me to look again at my life
> and see how far I've wandered from your virtuous way.

The Visitors warned Lot that Sodom would be destroyed and he must escape – now! Lot was seriously worried and prepared to leave, but still he vacillated. The Visitors had to physically force him to go, before Sodom was engulfed in fire. 'Flee to the mountains', they warned, but this was too arduous for Lot, who always wanted to take the line of least resistance. 'Look, here is a town near enough to run to, and it is small,' he bargained.

Lot's story had a truly horrible ending. After all the fuss he had made to be allowed to settle in Zoar, he got worried and did move up to the mountains. Isolated and abandoned, reduced to living with his two daughters in a cave, none of his choices had preserved him at all. Finally, the daughters tempted him into such drunkenness that he slept with them. Without a strong web of relationships, or a guide wiser than he, Lot's family descended into chaos and iniquity. Without strong bonds to support him, this weak man was ambushed by events; without understanding, this foolish man was forever a victim.

In the following weeks we will examine many relationships, some better than these, a few even worse, and ask ourselves what makes the difference between positive and negative outcomes to our choice. One obvious answer is what is conspicuous by its absence in the entire Lot story: never once did he pray.

> Lord Most High, there are times I must climb mountains
>   in a mist of doubt,
> and scale peaks with only trust as my guide,
> and set out not knowing what is on the other side;
> such is the nature of faith.
> Amen.

But we have the mind of Christ

1 Corinthians 1—2; Luke 6, 12

Where is the wise person? Where is the teacher of the law?
Where is the philosopher of this age?
Has not God made foolish the wisdom of the world?
(1 Corinthians 1.20)

It is certain that Jonah and Lot did not know the answer to this question. And still today there are plenty of candidates lining up to be counted as wise men and women. There are universities full of dedicated scholars. There are philosophers – some obscure, and others whose books fill the self-help shelves of our bookshops. Then there are the 'chattering classes' and newspaper pundits and politicians who chew over every twist and turn of our social ills. Yet still we go on making the wrong choices, individually and collectively. We go on wanting to be wise, but fool ourselves into thinking we can do this without embracing or experiencing change.

Not many of you were wise by human standards, not many
were influential;
not many were of noble birth. But God chose the foolish things
of the world to shame the wise. (1 Corinthians 1.26)

All we know of Jesus' background is that his first cradle was a manger, and his father was a carpenter; but we also know for certain that he consistently focused on the poor who had no voice. He concentrated his attention on eternity, not survival, on beauty and not wealth, on love and not on learning. Don't worry about your larder, your wardrobe, your bank balance, he said: look at the birds and flowers – such ephemeral lives, yet such splendour! Don't hoard food or influence, power or pleasure – these will all pass, unless you are 'rich towards God', as the rich fool was warned when he built huge barns to store his

11

wealth, only to be told 'This very night your life will be demanded from you' (Luke 12.16–21). Jesus' parables always make us look beyond our human standards.

> We do, however, speak a message of wisdom among the
>   mature,
> but not the wisdom of this age or of the rulers of this age,
> who are coming to nothing.   (1 Corinthians 2.6)

Why is it that some people hear these messages and others can't or won't? Sound waves penetrate our ears, pulse along the sounding strings that curl up in the snail-shell coil of our inner ear, until they make sense in our brain. But all sorts of seepage can occur within that labyrinth. There may be a rumpus outside so we don't quite catch every word; we may be distracted by the phone and so not concentrate. We may hear what we disagree with and reject it, or hear what puzzles us and say, 'I'll think about that later.' We may hear the message but believe 'that's quite right, but it doesn't apply to me'. The immature person has all these ideas, like the foolish builder who built his house on sand and didn't reflect on the deeper meaning of God's word, and so his plans came to nothing. The mature Christian is someone who 'hears my words and puts them into practice', like the wise builder who dug deep foundations into the rock (Luke 6.46–49). These people have the wisdom to know in what way Jesus' message does apply to them.

> The Spirit searches all things, even the deep things of God.
> For who knows a person's thoughts
> except their own spirit within them?   (1 Corinthians 2.10)

Soul-searching is a good part of what prayer is about; it is giving the time for God to speak to us and allowing a space for us to hear. The purpose of prayer is to magnify those sound waves and clear away all the background noise that distracts us.

> The person with the Spirit makes judgments about all things.
>   (1 Corinthians 2.15)

We are not meant to wander through life with a laissez-faire attitude. For Jesus wants us to learn to judge ourselves: look at the plank in your own eye, before you criticize the speck in your neighbour's. 'The student is not above the teacher, but everyone who is fully trained will be like their teacher' (Luke 6.40). And that is the gift of the New Testament – we have the mind of Christ as our trainer and our guide.

> God, supreme mind of the universe,
> Jesus, noble teacher of the truth,
> Spirit, wisdom of the Trinity,
> breathe into our hearts your word, your love, your wisdom.
> Amen.

WEEK 1: FATHERS

———◆·◆·◆———

Ask your father and he will tell you, your elders, and they will explain to you. (Deuteronomy 32.7)

A change of mind:
the Parable of the Lost Son

Luke 15.11–31

> Father God, when I make a life-changing decision,
> help me leave mere inclination behind
> and realize the danger of unexamined desire.

Some of us in life know exactly what we want, and others never really do. Our first story is of a young man who has no trouble knowing what he wanted, or going after it. We only ever make decisions on less than perfect information for we never know how things will work out. Life isn't an experiment which allows us to operate a control version. The younger son who asked for his share of the inheritance had the confidence of youth that all would work to his advantage. But the difference between being decisive and being headstrong is very fine indeed. Everything the younger son did, he did wholeheartedly, a quality we know Jesus wants us all to share. Think what it means to be 'wholehearted': your self is united and energized. But rather than controlling his passions, he allowed himself to be led by them. So:

> In a moment of calm, ask yourself:
> what am I wholehearted about?
> Is God part of it?

The story starts briskly: 'Father, give me my share of the estate' (v. 12). We don't hear the father try to dissuade him. But we can guess his trepidation and imagine his conversations with the young man's mother late into the night. How hard it is to watch our children make their own mistakes.

> Father, give parents the confidence to trust that if
> they let go of their son
> he may return as a man.

16

And indeed, after seeing his hopes collapse, and wandering in a wilderness of loneliness and destitution, 'he came to his senses' (v. 17). What a marvellous phrase it is, to 'come to our senses'. Our physical senses are the faculties through which we experience the outer world, but here it's used in the further meaning of reaching wisdom based on experience – the senses of our intellect and soul. He learnt to appreciate and understand the ramifications of his actions, accept his disappointments, and turn back to his father. Here is the second major decision he made, a decision that led to him becoming more like the person God really wanted him to be.

Of course, another word we could use for 'coming to our senses' is one we use a lot in Lent – 'repentance'. And it was the change within the son and the journey back that was more important than the speech, for the father, 'filled with compassion', forgave him even before he heard the words. Here is an image of our God and Father throwing his arms about us. The son did get to say his words of repentance but the father was too busy preparing the banquet of reconciliation to bother to reply.

> Father, when I need to repent,
> help me realize that actions speak louder than words.

Because we invest so much pride in our decisions, it's very rare for us to have a complete 'change of mind'. How often we castigate people and politicians particularly for making U-turns. We criticize people who 'climb down', when in fact maybe we should praise their 'climb up', for changing one's mind is as arduous and painful as climbing a mountain. Of course, it's not admirable to change if it's for short-term success, but if it's a genuine change of mind and heart, based on careful assessment of new circumstances, why should we be so critical? Youthful *ideals* are so important, for we must have a vision to live by, but often they become a fixed *ideology* which governs us, and we need shaking out of our obstinacy.

Can you remember what it was like as a child when you'd been rude or thumped your little sister, and dad told you to 'say sorry'? How very difficult it was to say the words, how much the heart rebelled and pride resisted. Do we get any better at apologizing as we get older? Not always, maybe not often, which is why we find the younger son so attractive – he's able to do what we so often find hard. The younger son travelled the journey we all make at some time of our life: he'd searched for fulfilment in the wrong way, he'd been hopelessly lost, but found wisdom in that wilderness, and was transformed.

> Ever-loving Father, bind fathers and sons together with
> trust and friendship.
> May the father be the pattern to the son
> and the son the delight of the father.
> Amen.

Joseph was a righteous man

Matthew 1—2; Hosea 11

The angel of the Lord said 'Get up.'
So must I leave behind all that is certain
and respond to your call.

If we look back at the Christmas story for a moment, we find that the 'star' in every nativity play is, 'of course', Mary, and the best supporting actor award goes to Joseph. But if we only had Matthew's Gospel, the roles might well reverse. In Matthew we learn nothing of Mary's response to the promise she carried in her womb. The focus is on Joseph and his relationship to the angel of the Lord, who visited him no less than three times.

God chose the earthly father of Jesus with as much care as he devoted to the search for his mother. Joseph was a righteous man, we are told, which meant at that time someone who kept the law and was what we'd call 'upright'. What is it that keeps us the right way up – like one of those children's wobbly toys that won't be knocked over, however often the toddler tries, and always bounces back up? We remain upright when we are stable enough not to be blown over by the ups and downs of life. When we have a centre of gravity in which our emotions, our mental outlook, and the guidance of God, all cohere, then our external experiences may rock us, but not overturn our stability.

So what influenced Joseph's thinking at this moment of crisis? The obvious decision, based on the expectations of his time, would have been to divorce Mary immediately. No one would have blamed him. But Joseph was not only righteous, he was compassionate. His reaction was not limited just by rules and laws, but broadened by empathy with Mary's predicament. Joseph held back from his initial impulse, and remembered his father's advice – sleep on it; things might look different in the morning.

While he was still tussling with this dilemma, his understanding was taken to a new level when an angel appeared in his dream with startling new information. The baby was, in a very special way, from God, and for a special purpose – to 'save his people from their sins' (Matthew 1.21). Through an inner experience, his insight was confirmed and Joseph took Mary home as his wife.

> The angel of the Lord said 'Do not be afraid':
> Give me courage to do the difficult thing, if it is right.

Joseph never swerved from the choice he'd made, and God continued to counsel him. Twice more an angel came at times of crisis, once to warn him to flee from Herod, and the final time when it was safe to return. Then he had to begin bringing up this special child. What guidance did he follow in his fathering?

Is it pure coincidence that we find one template for good fatherhood in Hosea 11? This is the very chapter Matthew quotes when he tells us of the Holy Family's return: 'Out of Egypt I called my son' (Hosea 11.1). In this passage Hosea gives a moving description of a loving father, equated to the Fatherhood of God.

> When Israel was a child, I loved him,
> and out of Egypt I called my son. . . .
> It was I who taught Ephraim to walk, taking them by the arms; . . .
> it was I who healed them.
> I led them with cords of human kindness,
> with ties of love;
> . . . I was like one who lifts a little child to the cheek,
> and I bent down to feed them.

Look at all those active verbs, showing just what hard work true parenting is! To father an upright child requires involvement and a sense of direction, away from wrong, towards good. It requires bending down to the child in humility and lifting him up to show him the distant horizon. It requires cords of love that hold the child, but loosely, with a readiness to release him when the time is right. It requires teaching and feeding, maybe not always with what the child wants to taste. And Joseph succeeded so well, that when at Golgotha the centurion observed his son, he concluded, 'Surely this was a righteous man.'

Righteous God, guide me along honourable paths,
teach me the ability to stand upright
even in a whirlwind.
Amen.

Listen, my sons,
to a father's instruction

---

1 Samuel 1—3

> I call out for insight
> and cry aloud for understanding;
> for knowledge which is more than facts
> and wisdom which is greater than thought.
> Above all, place into my heart an obedience
> that will direct the course of the just.
>
> (based on Proverbs 2.2–8)

Being told to do what your father tells you doesn't sound too convincing in today's world, does it; maybe not the best approach from a modern father to his son? But in Old Testament times there was a much more direct understanding of the respect a son owed his father, and the rights of the father to teach his son. And the value of this attitude was as part of a belief that we are all accountable for each other; that one person's foolishness or spite could devastate a family or society. It was obvious to them that if you were for God, God was for you – 'Do not forsake wisdom, and she will protect you' (Proverbs 4.6) – but if you turned away, disaster would follow.

> God of the family, when sons and fathers are at odds
> and go their separate ways,
> encourage them to turn and face each other again.

The story of Eli the priest describes the downward spiral unleashed by such disregard, but also includes a more subtle, contrasting theme. When we meet him in the Temple, Eli appears a gentle, kindly man, though a little short-sighted, mistaking Hannah's intense praying for drunkenness. Perhaps Eli spent too long 'in the office' and not enough time with his sons, for Hophni and Phinehas 'were scoundrels' and 'had no regard for the LORD' (1 Samuel 2.12). The order of the verses in Chapter 2 point to Eli's dilemma: one moment we are told, 'This sin of the young men was very great', and the next, 'but Samuel was ministering before the LORD': Samuel, Hannah's child whom she gave to the Lord, and whom Eli supervised and cared for (see also Week 4). Throughout the story we are shown the contrast between the wayward behaviour of Eli's natural sons and Samuel's obedience.

> Blessed are those who listen to me,
> watching daily at my doors,
> waiting at my doorway.
> For those who find me find life.
> (Proverbs 8.34, 35)

Were the sons jealous of Eli's attention to Samuel? Were they the victims of an absent father who only turned up to tell them off? In any event, they rejected their father despite his warnings: 'Why do you do such things? . . . The report I hear spreading among the LORD's people is not good.' Their actions were to cause wreckage like a multiple crash on a motorway.

While his sons 'did not listen to their father's rebuke', the boy Samuel 'continued to grow in stature and in favour with the Lord and with people'. How the brothers must have hated him!

When, on the other hand, Samuel heard the Lord calling him, he was convinced it was Eli, but Eli realized it was the Lord. When Samuel submitted and followed his instructions, the Lord spoke to Samuel, as he will speak to you too.

> May my prayer ever be:
> 'Speak, for your servant is listening.'
> (1 Samuel 3.10)

Once more the story turns to Eli's own sons, for God's warning to Samuel was of the disaster to befall Eli's family 'because of the sin he [Eli] knew about; his sons uttered blasphemies against God, and he failed to restrain them'. God leaves Eli no wriggle room at all; despite his efforts, his responsibility is not negotiable and his family line is wiped out.

How do parents instil their values into their children, or bequeath their love of God to them? If only we truly understood that process. It is easy – like the Old Testament God! – to pontificate and say it's by example and instruction, yet we all know families where there's a 'black sheep', where bewildered parents were no more negligent than the rest of us.

How great the responsibility of parenting is, and how little training we receive for it. We practise on the very children we are given to nurture.

> Father God, parent of the world, give to fathers wise words;
> Son Jesus, who loved the little ones, help children listen well
>   and gain understanding;
> Holy Spirit, who moves between heaven and earth, instil in
>   us your wisdom,
> and cement the bonds between the generations.
> Amen.

Two torn robes:
Samuel, Saul and David

1 Samuel

Ruler of kings and Master of shepherds,
help me recognize wisdom in the young as well as the old
for it is often found in surprising places.

Look carefully at these two robes, for they are very different – one
the worn and dusty garment of an old prophet, Samuel, the other the
richly embroidered cloak of King Saul. When we first meet Saul he
is 'an impressive young man without equal among the Israelites – a
head taller than any of the others' – as if wisdom and leadership can
be measured in metres! But, too soon, Samuel the prophet is rebuking
Saul for thinking he can 'go it alone' without Samuel's guidance. Samuel
wanted to be a father to Saul, and there are often times in all our lives
when people might act as mentor and parent, if we'd only let them.

We soon realize Saul is not at peace with himself or at ease with
God, for his deepest problem is that he doesn't understand his own
motives. When, in the aftermath of battle, Saul disobeys God's instructions, Samuel challenges him. Saul pretends he kept back the enemy's
flocks for sacrifice, but he can't pull the wool over Samuel's eyes.
Saul only acts from his emotions – love, rage, pain or fear – never
realizing that a feeling is not a thought. He is all ego – 'the unobserved
self' (Richard Rohr, *The Naked Now*, p. 90).

Mindful God, when I think with my heart,
help me observe my feelings and put ego aside.
Make me aware of my real motives.

Samuel bowed out of the story at this point – this was a mentoring
relationship that hadn't worked out. Too late Saul realized how much

he still relied on him, and he was terrified of having to take real charge of events. This tall, imposing king acted like a frightened child, begging Samuel to stay, and in his panic he grabbed hold of him, catching the hem of his robe with such force that he tore it (1 Samuel 15.27).

Soon afterwards, David came into Saul's life, as if God wouldn't leave him unsupported, and we embark on the heartbreaking story of a king who tries to father a rival, and a reluctant heir who acts like a son. Saul became locked into a love–hate relationship with David, for he soon owed him so much, including his recovery from the evil spirit which begun to plague him (we might call this his troubled unconscious), for it is only David and his harp that could soothe him (1 Samuel 16.23).

> Teach me to accept the help of others with grace
> and receive their love with gratitude.

It is natural in a father–son relationship that the power of the father wanes as that of the son grows. This is starkly evident in 1 Samuel 18 with the repeated chant 'Saul has slain his thousands, and David his tens of thousands', which enraged Saul. A wise father steps back – even if a little ruefully. A selfish father fights to maintain supremacy. Saul's behaviour was nearer to the instincts of the animal kingdom where only one dominant male is allowed in the pack. Impulsive as ever, Saul plotted to kill David. Once we fear someone, we no longer see the person, only an obstacle, or even an enemy.

Picture David hiding deep in a dark cave in the wilderness, when he hears a familiar voice at the entrance. Saul has unwittingly walked into David's hiding place. David could so easily kill the king but instead, he crept up on Saul unnoticed and quietly and deliberately and calmly cut off a corner of Saul's robe to prove what danger Saul was in. 'I will not lay my hand on my lord . . . See, *my father*, look at this piece of your robe in my hand!' (1 Samuel 24.10). This is the act of a merciful man, trying to mentor by his actions what Saul couldn't grasp in words. In a rare moment of clarity, Saul calls out 'Is that your voice, David *my son*? . . . You are more righteous than I' (v. 16). If only Saul had had the ability to listen so acutely at other times.

So, who acted more like a father – who was caring and forgiving, offering the other second and third chances when he revealed his weaknesses? Surely it was young David, and it was Saul who acted as an immature son, in his incapacity to think through the consequences of his actions.

> Father God, when I'm torn in two by my emotions,
> recall me to my rightful mind.
> Amen.

Abraham, father of nations

Genesis 16, 22

Loving God, look with kindness on all unhappy families.
Help them turn from jealousy and hurt
and learn to love again.

We think of the Patriarchs as giants, if not saints – Abraham, Isaac and Jacob working in harmony to fulfil God's plans; the revered founders of a nation. Father, son and grandson, bound together by legend and honoured by religion. But as well as being a founder of nations, Abraham was a father of two sons – individual, living, breathing sons. How good was he at that sort of fathering?

In some ways, the story of Abraham is a long, perambulating saga, paralleling Abraham's own wandering through the Middle East, under God's orders. How could it be told afresh today? If it were put on in the theatre, would it be another musical by Andrew Lloyd Webber? Maybe it's a subject for a fantasy film with visions and strange apparitions, sacred groves and kings whose armies threaten devastation – like *The Lord of the Rings*, replete with ponderous place names like Ellasar or Kedorlaomer.

It's got a touch of Wagnerian opera about it, too, full of drama and sacrifice. You can see the moment (in Genesis 16) when Sarah convinces Abraham to have a child through her servant, Hagar – there are the two of them, in the spotlight, centre stage, weaving a plan that the audience knows will end in disaster. For soon the plan turns sour, as Sarah's jealousy surfaces: 'now that she knows she is pregnant, she despises me', and Hagar must flee, only to be brought back by God. Abraham banished Ishmael, his true firstborn son, not once, but twice! The first time he's driven away in his mother's womb, the second time after Isaac's birth; both times to assuage Sarah's jealousy. You can hear Hagar's grief as mother and child are evicted from the clan, and face death in the desert without water, and she laments, 'I cannot watch the boy die.' Abraham loved Ishmael, his firstborn, but he couldn't protect him against his wife's viciousness. He's no example of a strong father.

> Father God, support and guide all families
> where there are stepchildren,
> and may each parent love them as their own.

Or maybe it's nearer a long Russian novel, closely observing the choices and tensions that Abraham and his sons face. As Tolstoy put it in the opening lines of *Anna Karenina*, 'All happy families resemble each other, each unhappy family is unhappy in its own way.' It's difficult to detect within the story on what basis Abraham made his decisions or whether he knew which was the better way; it seems he simply reacted to events and pressure from others.

Sadly the stories descend sometimes into soap opera in the way people behave and misbehave. In today's terms, we'd call Abraham's family dysfunctional; it's no good looking to him for an example of good parenting. Here we meet one of the underlying themes of the Old Testament – how the sins of the father descend down the generations:

> Man hands on misery to man.
> It deepens as a coastal shelf.

So said Philip Larkin in his poem 'This be the verse', usually more famous for another line, which is equally relevant to this piece! (See his *Collected Poems*.)

These stories could almost be morality tales to teach us how not to behave. Sadly but inevitably the tremors of rejection and folly will continue to rip through God's chosen family, and their relationships have no immediate hope of being repaired.

> Holy God, often we misunderstand your meaning,
> often we mistreat those we should protect.
> May we be resolute in raising our families
> and faithful to our responsibilities.
> Amen.

The Lord will provide

Genesis 22, 25, 27

God our Father, help us distinguish between true humility
and passive despair.
Train us in humility and release us from despair.

Isaac is an elusive character; every time we meet him, he is notable
for his passivity. First he appears as Abraham's son and sacrificial
victim, then, after a brief appearance as a vacillating husband (see
Week 2), he reappears as a feeble father who's easily tricked, and whose
dying wishes are thwarted. Our ideal of Christian humility sometimes makes us think that compliance and acquiescence are always
virtues. But though God asks us to trust him, he didn't intend us to
be doormats.

Isaac's only words in the story of him as son, when he is to be
offered as a sacrifice to God, are brief and pointed: 'The fire and wood
are here, . . . but where is the lamb for the burnt offering?' (Genesis
22.7). No more of the conversation with his father is recorded. But
surely Isaac chatted as they continued up Mount Moriah, if only
to comment on the view! Surely when Abraham took hold of him,
Isaac cried out in disbelief? How could the father who'd banished
the older son in his favour, now be planning to kill him? But once
the ram is caught and sacrificed in Isaac's place, Isaac speaks no more,
and is lost from the story.

What did they say to each other as they plodded back down the
mountain? Did Isaac understand and forgive his father, or did he
never trust him again? Isaac never appears as the subject of his own
life. The story is told only from Abraham's point of view, and even
then we don't know what he's feeling or thinking. We know he came
to believe that 'The Lord will provide', but did he explain this to Isaac?
Most of us identify with Isaac and not his father, and are dismayed

and amazed at the same time. What loving father would carry out this order? Though sometimes a parallel is drawn between the sacrifice of Isaac and Jesus on the cross, there is one huge difference: Isaac was a vulnerable child, relying on his father to protect him, while Jesus was an adult able to operate his own free will. Just giving up all participation in relationship because we rely on God's provision is an abdication of our human status.

> Provider God, give me eyes to see what you offer,
> and a heart to choose wisely.

Fast forward to the end of Isaac's story and he is now a father of twin sons. What has he learnt from his upbringing about the role of parent? He's seen his half-brother Ishmael banished in his own favour yet he's seen his father prepare to kill him. What a confusion he'd suffered between being loved too much and loved too little! We'd say that's enough emotional trauma to damage him for life. Indeed we are shown Isaac 'old and his eyes were so weak' (Genesis 27.1). How little insight he'd learnt over his long life. He certainly hadn't vowed 'I won't treat my kids the way my Dad did!' When Jacob plotted to usurp his elder brother, Isaac was initially rightly suspicious of the imposter, but he easily gave way and his regret came too late. We do not see a man growing in stature as he matures. All he seems to have learnt from his life is that he is at the mercy of other people.

> Without deeper insight, a strong will is dangerous.
> Without determination, our best intentions fail.

Twice in this family drama the focus is on the forsaken firstborn son. As Isaac replaced Ishmael, the symmetry of the story leads to grim justice when Isaac's firstborn, Esau, is usurped, and Isaac reaps what his father sowed. 'If you do not transform your pain, you will surely transmit it to those around you and even to the next generation' (Richard Rohr, *The Naked Now*, p. 125).

There seems no way out of this maze of betrayal. We constantly repeat the same mistakes, for we are still living with the consequences of the Fall. We must wait for Jesus to lead us out of the labyrinth of sin and despair.

Father God, we give thanks that you sent your son,
the son whom you loved,
to bridge all our divisions
and heal all our relationships.
Amen.

Good gifts: the Lord's Prayer

Luke 11.1–13

> Our Father, give us today our daily bread
> and all the other wonders you have in store for us.

Luke 11 starts where we all should – 'One day, Jesus was praying'. The disciples are at a distance, observing him discreetly. Is this in simple curiosity, or in awe? They can tell that when Jesus prays he's closer to God than when they recite their familiar prayers; they sense that when he returns from his times of prayer, he's changed, and uplifted, in ways they seldom are. So this time, one of them plucks up the courage to ask 'Lord, teach us to pray'. In today's language, whatever he's got, they want a slice of it.

The prayer he gave them we know, probably too well. Its simplicity makes it easy to say but so difficult to live by. Jesus knew his disciples well enough to know that they'd need some explanation, and in fact, the explanation is longer than the prayer itself! Jesus wanted more than anything to convey the loving nature of the Creator God. So the explanation doesn't go line by line, but to the heart of his relationship with God – one of Father and Son.

Jesus wanted to convince us that God's showering of good gifts goes beyond what a child *needs* to flourish. Loving fathers don't just give necessities – a fish or an egg (vv. 11–12), they give gifts – unnecessary blessings, the icing on the cake. I had a father – a daddy – who did just that. Every evening at 6.15 we'd listen for the key in the door, as he came home tired and sometimes late because of the traffic jam at Hammersmith Broadway. Mum had his place laid at the table and dinner ready in the oven. We, who were already full from our earlier tea, would break off from our homework to come and hug him, then we'd stand around the table expectantly, like chicks in the nest. He'd feed us titbits from his plate – the crispiest chip, the juiciest morsel of meat, the sweetest mouthful of pudding. He indulged us from his overflowing love.

> Thank you for the loving fathers that most of us are blessed with,
> and remind us to say thank you while there is still time.

'If you then, though you are evil, know how to give good gifts to your children', Jesus taught. We've seen some of the evil, earlier this week – fathers who'd give a snake or a scorpion – and know that our loving always falls short. In a way, it is our revulsion at people who harm and abuse children that proves the natural law of parental love. 'We were born with a consent to love' (H. A. Williams, *True Wilderness*, p. 110).

> Jesus, we bring before you all children forced to grow up too
>   quickly,
> the abused, enslaved or those trafficked for sex, whose
>   innocence is stolen.
> Bless, rescue and preserve them.

Jesus' teaching about giving good gifts is not just to help us work out how to be good parents. He speaks this way to show 'how much more will your Father in heaven give' (v. 13). Through the Lord's Prayer we make petitions and pledges, but the prayer would be null and void without the opening word 'Father'. That's why he continues with the glorious promise, 'Ask and it will be given to you, seek and you will find.' God is a father who longs to respond.

We know that prayer is more complicated than this, and that it's childish to believe we'll get everything we want in life, just as the child of a loving father learns that sometimes restraint and discipline must apply. It is our Father's role to teach us the difference between needs and wants, and he does this with us in this prayer. But we are left in no doubt whatsoever that the underlying impulse of the creator God is to give good gifts to his children.

> Generous Father, we praise you for your gifts of creation,
> of intellect and imagination, of family and friendship,
> the gifts you want us to enjoy on earth
> as well as in heaven.
> Amen.

WEEK 2: COUPLES

———◆———

And they become one flesh.
(Genesis 2.24)

Banished from Eden:
Adam and Eve, Mary and Joseph

———◆•◆———

Genesis 3, Matthew 1, Luke 1

Teach us Lord, the meaning of commitment,
the importance of honesty
and the value of trust.

Like the best of stories, both the Old and the New Testament open with
the tale of a young couple at the beginning of their lives together.
Will it turn out happily ever after? It is their choices which dominate
all that follows. The Old Testament choice – to work against God –
explains the tragedy of human reality, while the second – to work with
God – offers the best, or only, chance of rescue and salvation.

'In the beginning' Eve trusted the serpent too readily, and God not
enough. Mary, however, questioned the angel who came to her, and
was even 'greatly troubled' (Luke 1.29) before she was convinced. Only
when Mary was sure did she commit herself to an alliance with God.
It is Eve's folly which shows us how important is the distinction
between gullibility and trust.

Trust continues to be the vital ingredient in the next part of each
story. Adam trusts Eve too quickly and isn't prepared to think for
himself or help Eve reconsider. Joseph had a greater challenge and
was slower to trust Mary's version of her pregnancy until convinced
by the Lord in a dream (Matthew 1.18–25). There is a lesson here for
couples today who so often rush into relationships with so little knowledge of each other, only to find their trust is misplaced.

God, you partner us when we are alone;
bless us with enduring love.
When our relationships are flawed and damaging,
arm us with grace against harm.

We know very little of Adam and Eve once they left Eden. Perhaps they managed to patch things up and live in harmony of sorts. But it's easier to imagine recriminations flying thick and fast – 'It was all your fault!'. 'Well, you never stopped me!' Most likely the calamity acted like a worm in the apple, turning their relationship sour, then rotten. Mary and Joseph, on the other hand, are an example of a good marriage, Joseph putting Mary's welfare before his own, even when he doubted her. He knew that commitment means for better or for worse.

As time passed, both couples had children. Adam and Eve may have been a good and caring Mum and Dad, who were just unlucky in their son. Or perhaps bitterness between them acted as a perverse example to Cain and their disobedience was like a stone thrown into a pond, the ripples ever widening, gathering strength until they grew into waves of evil.

Mary and Joseph's parenting is more evident. From putting each other first, they learn to put their son, Jesus, at the centre of their lives, fleeing to Egypt to protect him. They did all the right things – moral, religious and practical – to provide for Jesus' growth. While Adam and Eve's sin was passed down to Cain, Mary and Joseph preserved Jesus' innocence.

Through Adam and Eve came the first death and murder which was handed down the centuries until it nailed Jesus to the cross. Mary, by now a widow, stood at the foot of that cross, bearing the pain alone. She had to witness the havoc Eve had let loose on the world millennia before.

Mary and Joseph could not stop that stone of evil, first tossed so carelessly by Adam and Eve, before it created a great storm; but it was their son, Jesus, who had the power to calm the waves.

> Loving Lord, be present in our loving partnerships,
> be the foundation as we build a relationship,
> be the compass as we journey together,
> be the welcome as we reach home.
> Amen.

Take her and go! Rebekah and Isaac

Genesis 24—27

> God, who is guest at every wedding,
> seal us together as one.

It is evening and a beautiful young woman steps lightly down the steps to the well, then, a few minutes later, reappears, a pitcher of water on her shoulder, careful not to spill a drop. Through kindness and custom she offers a drink to a traveller and even to his camels, which rest near the well. Trustingly, she accepts the gold bracelets he offers, and they jingle on her wrists as she runs to tell her mother and brother, Laban, of the visitor. When this visitor explains his task is to find a wife for Abraham's son, Isaac, Laban simply says, 'Take her and go, and let her become the wife of your master's son, as the LORD has directed' (Genesis 24.51).

Rebekah has unwittingly walked into her future, plucked out by Abraham's servant to become the wife of Isaac. By such a crossing of their paths, the saga of the Patriarchs continued. We can read and write this story as a romantic tale. On the other hand, we can say that Rebekah is dazzled by gold and scooped up by men, used as a transaction as if she were a fleece carted off to market. Of course, arranged marriages were the custom then, but as with so many women in the Old Testament, Rebekah never gets to tell her side of the story.

> Lord of the weak and silent, we pray for women who
>   still have no voice;
> teach men not to be afraid to let go of their power.

A word that's rarely spoken in the Old Testament is 'sorry', yet how necessary it is to healthy relationships. We can count the number of times sorry should have been spoken in Rebekah's life. Abraham gave no thought to the feelings of a young girl uprooted from a distant land to serve his will; Laban her brother gave her a choice which was hardly a choice – go now, or in ten days' time, he offered.

We are told that Isaac loved her, but his love soon looked pretty shallow. When the men of Gerar saw Rebekah, Isaac pretended she was his sister, not his wife, for 'The men of this place might kill me . . . because she is beautiful' (Genesis 26.7). His only concern was for his own safety; none for her honour. This was hardly an act of courage, and the only purpose being pursued here was Isaac's. But still no apology was heard. Had he learnt this disregard from his father Abraham's treatment of the women in his life, especially Hagar, the mother of his half-brother Ishmael, whom Abraham had banished?

> Deepen our awareness of the feelings of the other,
> and help us to test our actions according to your selfless love.

The catalogue of misbehaviour was contagious. For Rebekah the beautiful, Rebekah the innocent, Rebekah the silent, soon learnt from her new family that deceit carried no shame, and ambition trumped respect. At last she found a voice, and connived with her favourite son Jacob to cheat the eldest, Esau, of Isaac's final blessing. She allowed her devotion to become ambition, and her distorted love to rule unchecked. What happened to Rebekah after this? Was she proud when she heard how Jacob prospered, sheltering with his uncle Laban? Did she ever say sorry to Esau and become reconciled, or did she die alone, full of remorse?

It's not enough to say to ourselves that this ancient story has nothing to tell us today. It's so often the case that when we've taken a major decision that's hurt another, we have to justify it to ourselves, convincing ourselves our life is built on firm foundations. We dare not take a deep breath and confess we got it wrong, in case our carefully designed sense of self collapses. We're not brave enough to apologize and take the risk of becoming a new, better person.

> Lord, your will is for us to thrive in relationships of love.
> Give me insight to know when my actions have harmed another
> and the courage to say I'm sorry;
> then through the forgiveness of your Son
> may broken lives be mended.
> Amen.

I will show my love: Hosea

> God our Lover, in the face of betrayal, may we be forgiving,
> in the face of faithlessness, repair our bonds of love
> and open the door of hope.

If we want to look in the Bible for insight into our relationships, we'd probably look first in the Gospels. When challenged, Jesus upheld the Jewish law that marriage is a lifelong commitment (Matthew 5.32), and this is still our general hope, though much battered by experience. But his own lifestyle of wandering from mountain to lake, lake to city, city to isolated village, and his expectation that his disciples do likewise, was hardly conducive to happy marriages among them. We know Peter was married because he had a mother-in-law, but we can only guess what his long-suffering wife had to say about his continued absences. 'Why's your new friend more important than your family? How am I supposed to feed the kids if you're not earning?' We can hardly blame her.

> Sometimes I'm confused by conflicting responsibilities
> and don't know what my priority is.
> At such times, Lord, remind me to pause and pray.

So marriage guidance counsellors won't find obvious help in the four Gospels. And though the creation story itself puts the joining of man and woman as central to God's plan, 'and they become one flesh' (Genesis 2.24), the Old Testament as a whole, as we are seeing, is often about how not to conduct a relationship.

But help is on hand in the prophet Hosea, whose book begins with him using his personal experience with an adulterous wife to berate Israel for her waywardness. But a remarkable shift occurs, and a chapter of beautiful poetry and exaltation follows as, prompted by

God, he refuses to take the easy, acceptable decision of divorcing her. Hosea's big-heartedness shows us that walking away may not always be what God wants of us: 'The people in whom . . . the chain of pain, resentment, and retaliation is broken because their love is not damaged but continues undiminished, are people who take away the sins of the world' (J. Neville Ward, *Friday Afternoon*, p. 19). So, Hosea prepared to win back his wife, and in doing so, he sets out how to nurture and protect a successful relationship.

In the first place, there must be attraction: 'I am now going to allure her . . . and speak tenderly to her' (v. 14). A good relationship needs words and actions and symbols of affection.

> Bless those who are falling in love.
> Blow on this spark with your loving spirit
> that it may burn brightly.

Next, the relationship must be one of equality: 'You will call me "my husband", you will no longer call me "my master"' (v. 16). This leads to a covenant being formed between the man and the woman (renewing the covenant between God and Israel). 'I will betroth you to me for ever,' he declares (v. 19).

Hosea then lists the fundamental principles that sustain this commitment – justice and righteousness, love and compassion, and faithfulness (vv. 19–20). Our Bible uses these big words so much, that the enormity of their meaning can be diminished by their repetition. But their importance can be tested by looking at their opposites – injustice, hate, disdain and disloyalty always lead to misery.

Good relationships are not just about connections, but also about growth. Developing from allure and tenderness, commitment and equality, and built on righteous principles, comes response. In Hosea, God's joy is so great that even the skies and earth respond with new oil and wine – always symbols of plenitude. When two people really love each other, that love overflows and creates surplus.

> Loving Jesus, your life and passion embody what Hosea
>   learnt and taught:
> justice is not righteous without forgiveness,

faithfulness will not endure without perseverance,
compassion is not pain-free,
and love will sometimes break our heart.
Bless, guide and guard our relationships
and help us live them according to Hosea's example.
Amen.

A *widow until she was 84:*
Anna

Luke 2.36–38

Surely your goodness and love will follow me all the
   days of my life,
and I will dwell in the house of the LORD for ever.

(Psalm 23.6)

We never know what the weather will be like each day when we wake up – clear skies or drizzle, light breeze or storms? In the UK we moan and mutter about trivial blips in summer sunshine, so who knows how we would cope with earthquakes and tsunamis. Yet, despite this, we all grow up with an irrational expectation that life is predictable and benign – the sun will come out tomorrow, won't it? If we are lucky, life is gentle with us and we receive only minor knocks when we are young, which educate and strengthen us to sustain the harsher realities that accumulate with age.

The usual experience of bereavement is to lose first a grandparent, an elderly neighbour or even 'just' a pet. But if, while we are still young, we lose someone of our own generation – a sibling, a school friend, a lover – the shock is terrifying. Our world disintegrates and we are cast out into a parallel universe where nothing is stable and life is malign, our heart torn up and flung to the winds.

This is what must have happened to Anna – seven years only with her husband, then widowed till she was 84. There's no mention of how her husband died – perhaps he was a lot older than her, or perhaps it was a sudden illness or accident. Nor is there any mention of children and no account that she found 'happiness' again. She endured over 70 years alone, and we can only presume that, at least in the beginning, she was very lonely indeed.

> God of the lonely, may I become a channel of your
>   consolation
> to those who grieve,
> and an affectionate companion to people alone.

'All suffering is change that is felt simply to be loss' (J. Neville Ward, *Friday Afternoon*, p. 78), and of course death of a loved one is the greatest loss of all; no benefit can be put in the scales to outweigh the pain. The darkness blots out all sense of God's presence, all his impulse of love and all the vitality, curiosity and belongingness that is his will for us. Only in time, though the ache never quite goes away, are we led, through grace, to a new reality where we can begin to experience life in its fullness. The cycle of bereavement must be lived through before we can reconstruct a different life, but one that does have value. We come through the 'valley of the shadow of death', following a different map to a different destination, with fresh scenery and other companions; no longer leading the life we expected to, but finding that after the upheaval, though the landscape will always be different, beauty returns. And after the depression and discontinuity, a new identity can be forged.

We all need a purpose, a home, and a hope in life, and in time, Anna found all three. Her new purpose and identity was as a prophet; her new home was the Temple, where she worshipped 'night and day'; her new hope was in 'looking forward to the redemption of Jerusalem' (v. 38). Anna is proof that God has more than one possibility in store for our lives. For when Mary brought Jesus into the Temple in her arms, she didn't think bitterly 'that could have been me'. God had honoured her and kept his promises, and her anguish was replaced by joy. That's why we are told 'she gave thanks to God', for she had long been released from the chains of grief, free to embrace the goodness of life again.

> Thank you, God, that you release, rescue and heal
>   us from loss.
> Out of the greatness of your love, renew us,
> and grant us in time a new purpose, a welcoming
>   home, and hope once again.
> Amen.

You are the man!
David and Bathsheba

2 Samuel 11—13

Faithful God, lead me not into temptation
but deliver me from evil.

Imagine springtime in ancient Israel. The brief explosion of blossom is already over, and the land will soon be parched and cruel. David, the great king, is still the noble person we met last week, now even greater because of his victories. His troops are away at war, and, he's walking on the palace roof, restless and in need of air, in the glorious sunset. At that very moment, a little way off in the palace complex, he sees a beautiful woman.

Bathsheba's restless too, missing her husband at the front, and so she goes to bathe – perhaps she'll sleep better then. What fatal timing! For in this moment, David falls, as far as if he'd leapt from the tallest tower of his stronghold. Temptation, lust and arrogance expose David's weakness, and combine to bring David and his family to the brink of disaster. It only took a split second.

When I am on the brink of temptation,
be the still voice in my mind
and warning beat in my heart.

David had misused his power terribly, and acted totally improperly, driven by false passions which destroyed his ability to see the consequences of his intentions. Here in this story we meet the extreme betrayals that can ruin relationships. David turned into a man who'll not only covet and steal another's wife but also commit murder. How many of the Ten Commandments was he prepared to break! David destroyed not only his own honour and Bathsheba's reputation, but also broke faith with Uriah, his loyal soldier (by arranging for him to be put into certain danger and death).

'But the thing David had done displeased the LORD' (2 Samuel 11.27), and Nathan the prophet opened David's eyes to his treachery by telling him one of the most touching parables in the Old Testament, about the rich man with flocks and herds to spare, who steals a poor man's one little ewe lamb (2 Samuel 12.1). David was shocked by the story but his folly had so blinded him that he couldn't see it was about himself, so Nathan had to spell it out: 'You are the man!' Sin and greed and lust all diminish our insight until we only see what we want to see.

> When we covet, we put our pleasures first;
> when we are disloyal, we put ourselves first
> when we lust, we put our desire first.
> But your Son taught us to put the other first.

David's punishment was both swift and prolonged. Swift, because the child he had conceived with Bathsheba died. Prolonged, because God declared 'the sword shall never depart from your house' (2 Samuel 12.10). And so it turned out, as his family collapsed into a hell of rape, incest and fratricide. For the calamity was not only David's – the innocent are victims too. David's sin was amplified in the sin of his son Amnon – 'man hands on misery to man' – who raped his half-sister Tamar. When David heard about this 'he was furious' (2 Samuel 13.21). But he could take no action – he'd lost the moral high ground years before.

> Lord, help me examine my heart and discover
> what it is I crave today that isn't mine;
> help me identify the times when deceit casts me into a
>   wilderness
> and brings destruction to myself and others.
> Lead me to restoration through your Son, Jesus Christ.
> Amen.

If any of you is without sin: the woman taken in adultery

———◦•◦———

John 8.1–11

Merciful Father, may I never judge another,
for I only know part of their story.

Years ago the story of the woman taken in adultery might have sounded archaic, an example of harsher times, and unconnected with our own. But in the last few decades we have been reminded that in some parts of the world the punishment of stoning for adultery continues. We must be sensitive before we criticize another culture, and tactful when we do, but our imaginations recoil at the thought of the terrifying death of women 'caught' in adultery.

We pray that all societies will exercise wisdom,
responsibility and mercy in carrying out justice.

Bathsheba could have been a victim of this law, which made David's crime even greater; God punished them in other ways. The Old Testament imperative of retribution still affects our thought processes today. But compare the Old Testament emphasis on God's punishment with Jesus' measured silence. He's been confronted by the Pharisees, who've dragged a frightened woman in front of him, accused of adultery. Alone in a sea of men, she's shaking with fear. 'Now what do you say?' they challenge, trying to catch Jesus out between their own rules and the authority of the Roman occupiers. But Jesus sits there quietly. It seems for once he's at a loss for words.

Which godly standard do we really put our trust in? Though we call Jesus our Lord, when we are hurt or our ideas are threatened, we can often revert unwittingly to the old idea of a wrathful God, who's quick to judge. It's as though we feel our guilt must be answered with a punishment, and we forget what Jesus came to teach us – that without God's love, none of us would be innocent.

We know nothing of this woman's history. We don't know if she was a young girl desperately in love with someone her parents disapproved of, or whether she'd been coerced, or raped. Is she a victim, or a brazen whore? We don't know, and probably neither did the crowd. Jesus chose not to condemn her, without caring whether or not she'd repented, or even would repent. His great love compelled him to set her free, regardless of her response.

This is why this reading is chosen for Ash Wednesday in the Anglican appointed readings, for Jesus' passion, which is approaching, is a lesson in learning to love, not hate, and to forgive, not blame. Ash Wednesday ushered in the season when we are challenged to examine our consciences and reflect on our sins – not the sins of others.

> Spirit of wisdom, help me look back over my life, particularly
>   the last year,
> to remember my faults and commit myself to amendment.

Jesus responded to the Pharisees with 'let any one of you who is without sin be the first to throw a stone at her', for the attitude he hated above all else was hypocrisy. He'd spent a lot of time in his sermon given on the mount explaining this. And, one by one, it was the older ones that went away first. For as we grow older, we become more aware of the times we've let ourselves down and hurt others, acted shamefully or selfishly. We become more reflective and understand that life's not all black and white. Everything is greyer as we age, not only our hair!

So the crowd dwindled, starting with the older ones. And if we look carefully at the crowd slinking away, eyes lowered, who do we see leading them, dressed in the old-fashioned robes of a king? None other than King David, himself.

> Forgiving Jesus, make me more ready to forgive than
>   condemn,
> to understand than to blame.
> Through your mercy, release me from my sin.
> Amen.

Nowhere to lay his head: Jesus

Matthew 8.20

God of relationships, when I have no hand to hold,
place your hand in mine.

All this week we've been looking at various stages of married and unmarried life. One of the first things a couple does together, is to make a home and settle down. Adam and Eve had the ultimate address – the Garden of Eden! Mary and Joseph had a workshop, David and Bathsheba a palace, and Anna a temple. However grand or simple, we know our home by the security and warmth we feel when we close the front door.

Today's wedding present list is a catalogue of the house – what's needed for the kitchen, bathroom and bedroom. Then once you've moved in, you must decide how to decorate the sitting room, the hall, or how to plant the garden. But the Son of Man had 'nowhere to lay his head'. As an itinerant preacher, he never set up house or became one of a couple.

In our society, many more people are single than in previous generations. Half of all households in London are reported to be single occupants – students and young professionals enjoying a fast paced social life before they 'settle down'; the sadly separated, single parents who've lost their home; the kind, loving person who just never found the right partner; the older person, widowed after a lifetime as a couple, learning to live alone again, and the frail and confused who have had to leave their home and live their last years in a 'home'. And Jesus is still wandering somewhere among this great turbulence of people.

May our churches be welcoming and sensitive to those who
live alone
not by choice but by force of circumstance.

Especially, we pray for people who live in Homes with a capital H.
May they be treated with affection and dignity
so that they truly feel at home.

At the start of his ministry, Jesus was driven into the wilderness and experienced extreme homelessness. The memory of this time must have been vivid when he spoke the words 'foxes have holes'. He'd have watched the desert animals returning to their nests and burrows while he searched for somewhere to sleep. For forty nights he had no bed, no pillow, for forty mornings no breakfast, except that which he could forage.

Outcast Jesus, be with the homeless who shelter under
   railway arches
who huddle for warmth in doorways,
and spur me on to find a way to help.

The irony is that at this time when singleness is so common, the pressures of our society and media stress the couple more and more; dating agencies proliferate and people are left to feel incomplete if they aren't one of a pair.

But if we look at some of the great figures of Christianity, we'll see how many were single, often through deliberate choice. The desert fathers and members of the monastic orders spring first to mind, for they really understood the cost of following Jesus. St Francis in particular took this verse as his imperative. Once, when staying with a group of brothers, one of them referred to the place where Francis was sleeping as '*your* little cell'. '"Because you said it is mine, someone else will stay in it from now on; I will not," he replied' (Society of St Francis (eds), *A Sense of the Divine*, p. 62).

More recently, think of women like Florence Nightingale, moved by compassion to leave the comfort of wealthy Victorian society to risk her safety in the Crimean War, or Mother Teresa who shared the poverty of the homeless and dying of Calcutta. Think of Aung San Suu Kyi, the Burmese opposition leader who has sacrificed the joys of her marriage for the sake of justice, and whose home became a prison, where there could be no pleasure in 'being settled'.

We thank you for the lives of saints and moral leaders
who gave up intimacy and the chance of a home
for the sake of truth and charity,
who put the love of others before their own private
    happiness.

Finally, let us take strength from the life of Jesus himself. Though single, he was surrounded by companions whom he loved, and who loved him; though homeless, he took his family with him wherever he went; though never married, he never felt incomplete, because of his relationship with God. God loves us not as one of a couple, but as ourselves, as individuals. Could anyone have been more creative, more loving, more fulfilled, than Jesus?

Companion Jesus, I invite you to make your home with me,
    this Lent.
Amen.

WEEK 3: SIBLINGS

———◆———

How good and pleasant it is when God's people live together in unity! (Psalm 133.1)

Who are my brothers? Jesus

Mark 3

Bless, dear Lord, your family.
May it live in a house without walls,
and a garden without fences,
and may the gate always be open.

James was just furious – without Jesus, he was left in charge, now their father had died. He was so angry that Jesus had gone like that, leaving him to shoulder all the responsibility. 'He is out of his mind' he shouted when he heard what a spectacle he was making of himself (Mark 3.21). He'll end up bringing shame on us all, he warned. We must get him to come home!

Joseph was more thoughtful – he'd inherited his father's capacity for dreaming. He'd often talked with Jesus long into the night, sitting on the flat roof under the dazzling stars, debating the problems Israel faced – the dictatorship of Rome, the dominance of the Pharisees, the despair of the people. He'd listened silently when Jesus explained that though it seemed impossible for someone from such a family, he felt God's power in him, compelling him to speak out. Joseph had lain awake long after, worried for Jesus' safety, but more and more convinced that Jesus was special.

Judas went for the trip, old enough to know the family was divided, but young enough to look forward to the adventure. He hated his mountain home and wanted really to be a fisherman, so hoped he'd have a chance to go on a boat trip with one of Jesus' new friends.

Little Simon had no choice. He still went everywhere his mother took him. But even he knew his mother was quieter than usual, and he didn't like it when his brothers were so grumpy that they refused to play with him.

The unnamed sisters were left behind, under the watchful eye of an uncle.

* * *

So here they all were, Jesus' four brothers and his mother Mary, tired and dusty, hungry and thirsty after a day's scramble down the mountain to the lake. They were all feeling nervous – they knew how unpredictable Jesus could be, how likely to come out with a remarkable reply to the simplest question. James was all for going straight in and dragging him back to his duties. But Mary knew they'd have to tread more carefully.

They didn't have to ask their way to Jesus, they only needed to follow the crowds. Once they found the right house, it was overflowing with people and they couldn't even get inside, so they passed a message in, announcing their arrival.

Jesus would have guessed immediately why they'd come. He remembered only too well the tears of Mary, and how angry James had been when he'd left. Here was Jesus at the beginning of his ministry – he'd been baptized by John, survived the wilderness, and just begun to express his remarkable healing powers. He'd gathered his disciples and, just a few days before, had appointed twelve apostles. He had so much to do, and a deep conviction that he didn't have time to spare. He just couldn't let his family get in the way of his Father's will.

> Challenger Lord, when you set out new purposes for me,
> do not leave your work unfinished.

And that is why the four brothers didn't get to meet Jesus that night. James, Joseph, Judas and Simon waited with Mary a while longer before they realized Jesus would not come out to them. Disheartened, they went to a cousin's house to spend the night. Judas never got to go out in a boat. And how hurt they would have been if they had heard Jesus' sharp retort: 'Who are my mother and my brothers?' Joseph at least might have understood his next comment: 'Whoever does God's will is my brother and sister and mother.' They had yet to learn that though they weren't excluded from his family, they must share it with many, many others. Jesus opened wide his arms, and not just on the cross.

> Your family includes the Oxbridge don and the struggling
>   schoolchild,
> the Olympic athlete and the paraplegic,
> the opera star and the street entertainer:
> all are welcome, who hear your word and act upon it.
> And still there is room for me.
> Amen.

(Jesus' four brothers are named in Mark 6.3.)

Bless me too, father!
Esau and Jacob

Genesis 25—27; Luke 15

Our Father, help us keep our gaze on you;
never covet our brother's blessing
or measure our sister's fortune
lest you count our folly against us.

We don't have to look in the Bible for evidence that the relationship between brothers can be riddled with rivalry and false expectations. In 2010 it was headline news, as two brothers stood against each other to become leader of the Labour Party. It was extraordinary how many pages were dedicated to the competition, and even more amazing that it was taken for granted that the younger brother, Ed, had somehow betrayed the older one, David, by daring to challenge him. It seemed clear to all the journalists that Ed had no right to win.

Being the younger sibling myself, I bridled at these assumptions. The era of the 'heir and the spare' has long since passed, hasn't it? So what is it about being firstborn that makes you more deserving? Yet we are still uncomfortable when the natural order is reversed. It seems we've learnt nothing since the time of Esau and Jacob, Isaac's twin sons.

Picture those toddler twins, one blond, the other with a shock of red hair, rough-and-tumbling in the shade of the tent, like two lion cubs in light-hearted play, brooded over by their mother, Rebekah. But is the skirmish a mere light-hearted pretence, or it there something deadly serious just beneath the surface?

All children live with the fear that their parents only have a certain reserve of love, which is finite and preferential. All children need that love in order to survive, and are convinced they must grab as much as possible before it runs out. Younger children are obsessed with comparing their treatment – isn't their slice of cake smaller? Why did Mum kiss brother 'hello' first? Whose Christmas present is the best?

> Bless all brothers and sisters.
> May they co-operate in love, and not compete in fear.

The story of Esau and Jacob shows support for this instinctive belief that for one to prosper, the other must fail. Once Jacob had tricked his father Isaac into providing the blessing due to the elder brother, Esau, there was only a 'second-best' blessing left over for Esau. We see Esau slip forever into second place, on the periphery of all future action. '"Do you have only one blessing, my father? Bless me too, my father!" Then Esau wept aloud' (Genesis 27.38). This comes from the fear that love is finite and measurable. To live with that belief is to be in a place of shadows where danger lurks and we feel constantly threatened.

Consider another pair of brothers, this time the very different sons of the Father in Luke 15, whom we met in Week 1. One was Mr Reliable, the other Mr Restless. It really doesn't affect the meaning of the story ('he was lost and now is found'), that we know which was the younger one, but to Luke it was important. For Luke's story disproved the notion that parents only have a restricted pot of love, and also insists that our place in the family is of no consequence, for each of us is of equal value. In this story, we see a father demonstrate he has enough love for both his sons, the feckless younger one and the obedient stay-at-home firstborn, and more to spare. 'My son, . . . you are always with me, and everything I have is yours' (Luke 15.31). To be in this relationship is to be in a sunlit place without fear.

> Brother Jesus, your kingdom will reverse all my ideas
>   of order and hierarchy.
> I cannot trick my way into your blessing,
> or earn entry by obeying orders.
> Help me treat others with the inclusive generosity
> you lavish on each one of us.
> Amen.

Now Laban had two daughters: Leah and Rachel

Genesis 29—35

God of our youth, our maturity and our ageing,
through all the stages of our lives, help us
to live in harmony with one another and ourselves.

The eldest, Leah, wasn't attractive. She had weak eyes, maybe even a squint, and it caused her to peer out at the world, looking permanently cross. The younger, Rachel, had eyes that sparkled with gaiety. She radiated confidence and happiness; life was going to be good to her. After snatching his father's inheritance from his older brother and ruining Esau's future, Jacob had fled to the safety of his uncle Laban, far away in Haran. What he was not counting on was that he'd fall helplessly in love with the first woman he met, who turned out to be Rachel. But Jacob was tricked by Laban into marrying Leah, the eldest, instead of the love of his life. Luckily for him, his was a polygamous society, so eventually Rachel became his wife too. But that solved nothing.

It's easy to blame Jacob for everything that went wrong between the sisters, but that is probably unfair. Leah held the power of being the eldest, but Rachel's power was in her beauty. And then the tables turned, for Leah discovered another power – her fertility, and Rachel discovered that all the beauty in the world couldn't bring her the one thing she wanted most – a child. The dramatic balance in these Genesis stories is exquisite and heartbreaking.

When did these two women first begin to grow apart? Possibly when they realized how different they were. Even among young children, you'll hear one say, 'Oh, she's the brainy one', or 'It's not fair, I wish I had her lovely blond hair.' We all have to learn to navigate the possibilities that life presents us with, and decide what's within our reach, and what is sheer fantasy. We each carry hopes in our hearts, and the mature person accepts they cannot all be achieved.

> Each of us is made in your image, yet each of us is unique.
> Give us wisdom and grace to find fulfilment
> in the gifts you have given us.

And where is God in this entire story? He tried to recompense Leah for being so unlovely and unloved. 'When the LORD saw that Leah was not loved, he enabled her to conceive, but Rachel remained childless.' Leah had son after son after son, and with each birth her hopes rose that, this time, Jacob would grow to love her. But each time her hopes were dashed. Imagine the tension in the family, with Leah and Rachel glaring at each other across the compound, grinding their teeth as they ground the flour for bread. Rachel, who had never previously had cause to resent her sister, settled for second best – Jacob's child through her servant. 'I have had a great struggle with my sister, and I have won,' she crowed, but her triumph did not last long. We are back in the realm of TV soap. Though the rivalry of Leah and Rachel is not as well known as that between Esau and Jacob, Leah and Rachel's bile was inherited by their many sons, and erupted in the plot against Joseph. We can't isolate hatred. Unloving is not neutral; it is always destructive.

We will never know what might have become of Leah and Rachel in their old age, when their fertility had passed and their looks had been lost by ageing skin and shrinking bones. We'll never know if they might have become reconciled by the equality of decline, and rediscovered a sisterly affection. For when Jacob's exile was over and he returned to the Promised Land with his tribe of sons (and one daughter, Dinah), Rachel was pregnant again, for only the second time in her life. But Jacob's return was to be blighted when Rachel died in childbirth and was buried in Bethlehem. Leah's death was not recorded, and her grave is unknown. It was Rachel's son Joseph who was to save the family from famine in Egypt; but it was Leah's son Judah from whom the great King David was descended.

Siblings

God of Sarah and Rebekah, Leah and Rachel,
none of us knows what part we play in your promise.
May we live in trust that each has a contribution to make.
Bless both our successes and our disappointments,
and through your providence, bring good out of tribulation.
Amen.

Brother Head and Brother Heart: Andrew and Peter

John 1.35–42; Acts 2

Jesus our brother, may each in our own way follow you,
and each with our best selves serve you.

Simon Peter speaks:

'It's the oldest meant to look after the youngest, isn't it? Dad was always saying, "I'm relying on you to keep an eye on him, Peter." And while Andrew was little, I generally did. I remember carrying him home on my back that bitter January day when he fell into the lake; his teeth chattered and his clothes were dripping wet. Mum, of course, told me off, which I didn't think was fair.

'But as we got older, it was Andrew that looked after me, really. He always was more thoughtful and sensible. He often seemed to go off into a dream, sitting by the shore, trying to see beneath the waves, as if trying to work something out. He was the calm and quiet one. A jolly good fisherman too, more patient than I. He'd sit for ages in the middle of the lake. "If the fish are here, Peter," he'd say, "we can't rush them. The Temple wasn't built in a day."

'That evening I'd left him near the shore, staring out over the hills beyond, as if there was a secret wrapped in the sunset. So when he came bursting into the house, we were amazed at the change in him. He strode into the room where Dad and I had already started supper, and began dragging me off the rug. "You've got to come, Peter, this minute, come and meet him. I've found the Messiah!" We thought he'd gone crazy. "Come and see for yourself, it's Jesus from Nazareth – he's more than a man, he's a moment in history. When he speaks, his words answer everything I've ever wondered about. It's as if I'm a fish caught on his hook. I've wriggled, but I can't get free. I've got to go with him, and so must you!" Dad's jaw dropped, and Mum started howling. It was so out of character; more the sort of thing I'd do. It was about the longest speech he'd ever made.

'I owe him so much.'

Jesus, teach me the wisdom to be found in thoughtfulness,
in quiet sitting and waiting for your truths to settle in my heart.

Andrew speaks:

'I suppose you always want to be like your eldest brother, always desperate to do what he's allowed to do. That first time he went out night fishing with Dad, how I wanted to go too! Most of the time he kept an eye on me, and let me hang around with his mates. But sometimes he was moody, he'd growl at me to go and amuse myself, and get out from under his feet. I knew then to let him simmer for a while – he'd soon come back to being kind, he could never keep cross for long. Hot or cold, Peter was, never lukewarm. He was so strong-headed, you see, always latching on to some crazy idea or another. He was a great one for arguing before he got all the facts. Sometimes I'd despair – "Oh Peter," I'd say, "if only you'd think before you speak!" But his heart was always in the right place.

'Once I'd taken him to meet Jesus, he knew what I was talking about, and became completely devoted to him. For a time I was even a bit upset, when Simon tried to monopolize the Lord, even though if it hadn't been for me, they'd never have met. But then I realized it was just like Jesus kept on saying, "Anyone who wants to be first must be the very last" (Mark 9.35). And anyway, Peter's heart was big enough for both of us.

'But did you hear his speech yesterday? I stood there and felt so proud. "That's my brother there," I said to the man from Phrygia (or was it Pamphylia?) standing next to me. We were all agog. I thought when Jesus died I'd never hear words like that again. It's just as if Jesus was talking through Peter. They were so close, that's not a fanciful thought at all.'

Spirit of Pentecost, awake my soul with dreams and visions,
that I may prophesy your word
and prove the wonders of your kingdom to the world.
Amen.

Please, God, heal her! Moses, Aaron and Miriam

Numbers 12

When we have power, keep us merciful;
when we are slighted, keep us open-hearted;
may petty resentment never corrupt love.

We don't know who the eldest was, but certainly Moses was the leader. Escaping slaughter as a Hebrew baby, he was brought up as a noble Egyptian, but knew of his heritage and felt loyalty to his people. As a young man he was passionate, even to the point of murdering an Egyptian who abused the Hebrew slaves. Already he was showing concern for the weak, but it was only after he had retreated to the countryside and become a shepherd that his true potential developed. Alone in the pasture all day, he grew closer and closer to God, until only a very thin skin separated them.

By the time Moses was sent by God to rescue the Israelites from Pharaoh, he had met up again with his brother Aaron and sister Miriam, and they appear a united family, working together as a team. It was to Moses that God revealed his plans, but when Moses protested 'I have never been eloquent' (Exodus 4.10), God remembered his brother Aaron: 'I know he can speak well'; so Aaron become his right-hand man.

The third member of the family got less attention – she was only a woman, after all! But Miriam was there to sing to the Lord when the Israelites escaped Pharaoh, and the Red Sea parted (Exodus 15). Described as a prophetess, she certainly led in worship. The family's reputation was at its highest, and nothing appeared likely to disturb their peace.

Head of the family, help us love our siblings for themselves,
and be glad at the others' successes,
and rejoice with their good fortune,
and seek always their well-being.

But no family is perfect, and though not as divided as the Patriarchs' in Genesis, their relationship faltered. The catalyst was such a minor thing: their dislike of their sister-in-law, Moses' wife. At first it was probably just a raised eyebrow, followed by a sigh whenever they met up, but soon their animosity spilled over into opposition to Moses himself. How often it's the case that a major gulf can develop from something that starts out small. What had been a united trio now suffered from the strains of jealousy and competition. 'Has the Lord spoken only through Moses?' they muttered. 'Hasn't he also spoken through us?' (Numbers 12.2). The squabble led to dire consequences when God summoned all three to the Tent of Meeting. There God spoke from a pillar of cloud, and declared the primacy of Moses: 'With him I speak face to face.' Miriam, on the other hand, was afflicted with leprosy.

The family could so easily have fallen apart at this point, but the horror brought them to their senses. Beneath their dispute, family bonds resisted the threat. First Aaron pleaded to Moses, 'Please, my lord, I ask you not to hold against us the sin we have so foolishly committed.' So Aaron acknowledged Moses' pre-eminence, and stood in solidarity with his sister. Then Moses cried out to the Lord, 'Please, God, heal her!'

Harmony was restored and a healing of the bonds followed the healing of Miriam's disease. The love within the family reasserted its power. And everyone learnt something that contributed to their wisdom. Miriam learnt that she was loved. Aaron learnt humility. Moses had chosen the right response, rejecting the temptation to punish and exclude, but seeking to restore Miriam to wholeness and mend their torn relationship. Moses already knew from his meetings with God, that he was 'the LORD, the LORD, the compassionate and gracious God, slow to anger, abounding in love and faithfulness' (Exodus 34.6). And if these were the qualities of God, his prophet could be no less.

Therefore, if you are offering your gift at the altar
and there remember that your brother or sister has
   something against you,
leave your gift there in front of the altar.
First go and be reconciled to them.
Amen.   (Matthew 5.23–24)

Cain was very angry, and his face downcast: Cain and Abel

Genesis 4

> Be alert and of sober mind. Your enemy the devil
> prowls around like a roaring lion
> looking for someone to devour.
> Resist him, standing firm in the faith.
>
> (1 Peter 5.8–9)

The field was rolling and recently ploughed. Two men stood at the top of the slope, silhouetted against the wide sky, troubled by brooding clouds. One of the men stooped to the ground, and when he rose again, he was grasping a large, jagged rock. After that, it was best to look away.

> Grieving God, forgive that fateful act
> in which we learnt to hate our kin,
> and kill, and not be kind.

Cain's trouble had started years ago, when his younger brother Abel had been born, and he'd begun to compete for his parents' love. But the real trouble came when he begun to compete with his brother for the love of *God*, over which form of sacrifice was most pleasing, and which would bring them nearer to his presence. The conflict had reached boiling point by the time God warned Cain: 'Sin is crouching at your door; it desires to have you, but you must rule over it' (Genesis 4.7). Like any good parent, God was laying a steadying hand on Cain's shoulder.

And that was when Cain made his worst mistake of all – he stopped listening. If only! If only Cain had paused; if only Cain had *replied*: 'Lord, how am I supposed to know what's right? You turned your nose up at my offering for no apparent reason. I didn't have an animal to sacrifice like Abel – I'm not a shepherd.

'Abel's been nothing but a torment to me since he was born. Everything was fine when it was just the three of us, Mum, Dad and I. They doted on me, till he came along with his sharp elbows just where he wasn't wanted. And then I was told to look after him! I wish he'd never been born.

'And what is this sin that's crouching at my door? I wish you'd speak plainly. You make it sound like a hyena howling for my blood. But you're so distant, so unattainable, and even when I try, you spurn my sacrifice. I don't understand what you want of me. Sometimes, when I'm in the fields and the green corn has just sprung up, I feel part of a greater glory, and look over my shoulder for you. You're never there.

'When I get angry, my blood boils, and my ears ring with my pounding heart and I can't think straight. Tell me how to master that!'

> When sin crouches at my door restrain me, Lord.
> When evil prowls around me, help me hear your voice.

And God might have answered:

'Dear Cain, stand back for a moment. Don't you realize you are more angry with me than with your brother Abel? It's all right to say so. What is anger, after all? It's your panic that events are beyond your control, your despair because they aren't predictable. Learn to govern your emotions in the same way as you direct your field hands in order to bring in the harvest. Now you are a man you must realize you are more than your feelings – that's what I mean by mastering sin. You always have a choice – that's what I call free will. Your head is for thinking, your heart for loving – use both.

'I know I don't always seem to be predictable. And sometimes I even appear to act unfairly – you won't be the last of my children to complain of that. But you are only seeing a very little part of my plan; it calls for patience and a perspective you can't see from your small field. My plan is most of all about sharing, and that is why you have a brother, so that you learn to share, as I have shared with you.

'This is the conversation I've longed to have with you. Let's talk again quite soon. Please, please don't banish yourself from my presence – I'd always miss you. You know I really do love you no less than Abel.'

God, you are everywhere and present in everyone;
be with me this Lent.
When I feel rejected and your presence is obscure,
stop me from wandering away into the hell of your absence.
Amen.

Am I my brother's keeper?

1 John 2—4

> Anyone who claims to be in the light but hates a brother or sister
> is still in the darkness. Anyone who loves their brother and sister
> lives in the light, and there is nothing in them to make them
> stumble. (1 John 2.9–10)

Of course, we know Cain never had that conversation with God which
we imagined yesterday. Cain never returned from the wilderness
he'd driven himself into, and never gave himself the chance to be
transformed. The conversation he did have with God – after he had
killed his brother – was very different, his guilt transparent in the
words he blurted out: 'Am I my brother's keeper?' (Genesis 4.9). The
New Testament answer is a resounding *yes: indeed*, you are your
brother's keeper, helpmate, supporter, carer and guardian. And for
those of us who have the mind of Christ in our hearts, the standard
is set far higher than it was for Cain.

> Anyone who hates a brother or sister is a murderer.
>
> (1 John 3.15)

The word *indeed* used above is deliberate. Look at how it is formed,
from two words, *in* and *deed*. In other words, we prove our love by
our actions.

> Dear children, let us not love with words or speech
> but with actions and in truth. (1 John 3.18)

What we have seen this week, especially in the Genesis stories, is that
hatred and love are a matter of choice as well as feeling. And the
choice is always a moral one, but often obscured by our inability to
understand how unbridled emotions can drive us to destruction. Cain
feared God, but not in a mature way; Jacob feared obscurity, Leah

70

feared loneliness, and Rachel feared her barrenness. However, we are promised:

> There is no fear in love. But perfect love drives out fear.
>
> (1 John 4.18)

In the wonderful hymn of love in 1 John 4, we are given the promise that 'God is love', but this lays a responsibility on us to respond. It is almost a form of covenant.

> Dear friends, since God so loved us,
> we also ought to love one another.   (1 John 4.11)

This love of our brothers (and sisters, and neighbours, and strangers, and even enemies, as Jesus repeatedly taught us) must be a practical love. At the very least it may require us to give love through compassionate aid and support.

> If anyone has material possessions
> and sees a brother or sister in need
> but has no pity on them,
> how can the love of God be in that person?   (1 John 3.17)

At the furthest extreme, it may require far greater sacrifice:

> This is how we know what love is:
> Jesus Christ laid down his life for us.
> And we ought to lay down our lives for our brothers and sisters.
>
> (1 John 3.16)

Our spiritual self and our experience of holiness cannot be wrapped in cotton wool, or sealed away from our daily lives and social interactions. If we fail in the day-by-day incidents, our souls will become grubby and soon stop reflecting God's light. We meet the divine in the muddle of humanity.

> For whoever does not love their brother or sister, whom they
>   have seen,
> cannot love God, whom they have not seen.   (1 John 4.19)

Only when the barriers of hatred and suspicion are finally broken down will we meet ourselves as fully integrated human beings.

Then we will see that we were looking in the face of God all the time.

> See what great love the Father has lavished on us,
> that we should be called children of God!
> And that is what we are!
> ... We know that when Christ appears,
> we shall be like him, for we shall see him as he is.
> Amen.   (1 John 3.1–3)

WEEK 4: MOTHERING

—•◆•—

And a sword will pierce your own soul too.
(Luke 2.35)

Mothering Sunday:
I will carry you: the God of Isaiah

Isaiah 46, 49, 66

Loving God, loving Mother, bless all those whom I carry in
   my heart.
May I mother them in your name.

'A mother's caring is the closest, nearest, surest, for it is the truest,'
said Dame Julian of Norwich seven centuries ago. That's why she knew
that 'As truly as God is our father, just as truly is he our mother'
(R. Llewelyn (ed.), *Enfolded in Love*, pp. 35, 36). Yet still today we find
it difficult to pray to God our Mother, our maker who bore us out
of love, as well as to God our Father.

Loving Mother, enfold us in your arms,
care for us with your compassion,
and watch over us with unending love.

One way we describe a pregnant woman is to say 'she's carrying a
baby'. And she goes on carrying all her life. That is the practical, active
way she proves her caring. In pregnancy, it's a permanent state, for
never for a second can she put down her load, which gets heavier
with every passing day.

Loving Mother, bless all pregnant women.
Keep them healthy and bring them to safe deliveries.

Once the baby is born, a relationship is formed which is very rarely
broken. The mother still carries the child, rocking her in her arms to
drive away the cries, cradling him as she feeds him, tentatively putting
her down in her cot but always hovering nearby, ready to scoop the
baby up again. In recent years we've got used to seeing mums in the

High Street carrying their babies in the slings of other older cultures, which bind the baby to their bodies so that they appear as one. And in just this way, God has strapped us close to her heart.

Dame Julian wasn't the first to state the obvious about the motherhood of God. Back in the early history of Israel, when patriarchal attitudes were at their strongest, the prophet Isaiah understood that God is our mother and knew the constancy of the care she carried:

> A load on me from your birth, carried by me from the womb:
> till you grow old I am He,
> and when white hairs come, I will carry you still;
> I have made you and I will bear the burden,
> I will carry you and bring you to safety.   (Isaiah 46.3–4 NEB)

Parents of adult children continue to suffer with and for them. If they are sensible, they suffer in silence, for the children want independence. But God's promise is that we remain her children even when we have white hairs. God will never relinquish the load she lifted when she created us, for 'I have engraved you on the palms of my hands', (Isaiah 49.16). She knows we'll meet all kinds of terrors in our lives, and risk many dangers, and even suffer tragedies, but 'as a mother comforts her child, so will I comfort you', she promised (Isaiah 66.13). We should not let our religion keep us as infants, but when disaster strikes, it is wonderful to be able to turn to the arms of our God.

> Loving Mother, we pray to you for all who carry the burden
>   of motherhood:
> shield and protect the mothers of war-torn lands
> that they may safeguard their children in peace
> and send them to war no more.
>
> Preserve all mothers in countries where natural disasters
>   wipe out homes
> and drive families apart.
> Bring them to safe shelter.

Enrich the mothers of Africa and other poor countries,
that they may lead their children out of poverty
and educate the future generation.

Support all single mothers who struggle to care for their
    children;
bless them and give them supportive family and friends.

Help all these mothers know they share their load with you.
Amen.

And she lived with her mother-in-law: Ruth and Naomi

Ruth

> God our Mother, bless the brave, the compassionate,
> the steadfast women of our world.
> Give them refuge under your wings
> and the assurance that they are cared for.

What a terrible fate – to have to live with your mother-in-law! She is the butt of many jokes, but the jokes reveal a real unease about this relationship which can be fraught with jealousy, incomprehension and possessiveness. So why would Ruth have risked going with her mother-in-law to a strange land?

> God our Mother, bless all mothers, mothers-in-law and
> daughters.
> Deepen their relationships and teach them the lesson of
> patient love.

In today's more equal world, we might find Ruth's submissiveness a bit uncomfortable. But what Ruth teaches us, which is still relevant today, is the virtue of steadfastness. Ruth is a Moabite, not Jewish at all, and there had long been opposition between the two neighbours. During a lull in hostility, a Jewish woman called Naomi married a Moabite and had two sons, each of which in turn married a local girl, one of whom was Ruth.

So far, Naomi's world was full and complete, her life turning out just as any woman would have wished for in those days. But her husband and then both their sons died without offspring – an absolute calamity for women in that society. To cap it all, there was a famine in the land.

The disaster was great for Naomi for she was beyond childbearing age, and without any prospect of children she returned to her Jewish family, declaring 'I went away full, but the LORD has brought me back empty.'

The story we read in the book of Ruth is a journey from despair to happiness, emptiness to fullness, and destitution to security. And Ruth's startling decision to leave her home and return with Naomi is the catalyst which provides the opportunity for renewal and rescue. Ruth's key decision released them from the chill of isolation and allowed hope in, like opening a window on the first day of summer.

> Compassionate God, let tears of love melt the ice of despair,
> and the soft dew of morning wash away our winter of pain.

To answer our first question, why would Ruth have gone with Naomi: surely because Naomi's suffering had opened Ruth's heart. Her surprising decision had far-reaching consequences which we see later when Ruth remarries and becomes the ancestor of King David. The story of Ruth proves that participation in God's kingdom is not restricted by borders but is reserved for those willing to respond. Ruth knew that belonging is important but can be by choice and not by blood.

'Where you go I will go, and where you stay I will stay. Your people will be my people and your God my God,' Ruth declared (Ruth 1.16). Ruth chose Naomi as her mother, anticipating Jesus' stern question 'who is my mother?' (cf. Mark 3.33). She had reached a level of wisdom that allowed her to make a bold decision, putting aside her natural fears; one that carried with it the possibilities of real growth, and not just for her, for it also transformed those around her.

Where did she learn such steadfastness, such compassion and such bravery? Surely from her own mother, for we learn by example. It's no good sitting a child down and saying, 'Now I'll teach you the meaning of the word compassion.' What you must do is act compassionately and in time the child will understand. We often hear people say, 'I never realized how much my mother sacrificed for me till now.' All the big words we Christians use – almost glibly – like righteousness, justice, sacrifice – can only be understood when we meet them in reality. Ruth, one of the untutored, little people of history, marginalized by her widowhood and ethnicity, knew these virtues in her heart and soul, and they informed her life. She embodies the Christian imperative to put another before oneself, and before the expectations of the world.

> God our Mother, our lives might be barren but your love
>   will fill us.
> We might fear we have no future
> but you always offer us new beginnings.
> Amen.

It is not by strength that one prevails: Hannah

---

1 Samuel 1—2; Luke 2

> Do not keep talking so proudly
> or let your mouth speak such arrogance,
> for the LORD is a God who knows,
> and by him deeds are weighed.   (1 Samuel 2.3)

Let us meet one of the many barren women whose stories are told in the Old Testament. Hannah's humiliation was vivid, visceral and raw, and her pain palpable. She was taunted by her fecund co-wife – year after year – till she languished in a dry desert of despair. Despite her loving husband's protestations 'Don't I mean more to you than ten sons?' she suffered an emptiness she could not endure.

> Lord, we pray for all women who long for children,
> and for women who endure miscarriages and stillbirths.
> Bring them comfort in their emptiness, and renewal in
>   their lives.

Hannah 'prays to God in her heart' and promised that if she conceived a son, she would dedicate him as a priest. And when God did bless her, she carried out her pledge, taking three-year-old Samuel to live with Eli in the Temple. It must have upset her so much to leave him there, perhaps hardly ever to see him again, and give up the mothering she had so longed for. Was she tempted to break her promise? It was a decision made at the height of emotion, but she didn't pretend that that rendered her vow invalid. She had the self-control to hold firm to her original decision. 'Therefore I have lent him to the LORD' (1 Samuel 1.28 RSV).

Other translations say 'I give him', but either way it's not really for the mother to give or to lend. All mothers know that their children are a gift, entrusted only for a term before they reach independence. We watch them grow and change, surprise and perturb us, and sometimes even hurt us. But God doesn't borrow them back like a book from the library; parenting is a shared effort. Both the earthly parents plus our heavenly Mother are required for the full nurturing of a new human being.

> Loving Creator, we thank you for the gift of children.
> Bless us in our task of mothering,
> and always keep us mindful that our precious child is lent
> by the Lord.

After Hannah handed Samuel over to Eli, she did not turn away in tears, as might have been expected, but burst out in a glorious song – a song which Mary of Nazareth borrowed hundreds of years later when she too was graced with a miraculous birth. What is amazing is how both these ordinary women are so extraordinary in their vision of God's relationship to power, as they connect their personal joy with the great reversal of the world that is her will. If only the strength of a mother's love could rule the world, all the predictions in their songs would come true. For they proclaim that if God can deliver this miracle to them, surely she can also arm those who stumble and ensure that those who are hungry are hungry no more. God so honours the role of mothering that she will scatter the proud and bring rulers from their thrones. If only we would accept once and for all Hannah's wise words: 'It is not by strength that one prevails' (1 Samuel 2.9), then we could delight in our deliverance from this world's authority.

> God of the little people, the overlooked, and derided,
> deliver us from the proud and the powerful.
> Help us recognize the value hidden in the insignificant
> and the strength within the simplicity of a mother's love.
> Amen.

Take this baby and nurse him for me: Moses

-------•◦•-------

Exodus 1—2

He took a little child whom he placed among them.
Taking the child in his arms, he said to them,
'Whoever welcomes one of these little children in my
name welcomes me.'   (Mark 9.36, 37)

The story of Moses' childhood is one of violence, grief and cunning,
a story full of determined, independent women, who work together
in adversity to rescue a little child. Its beginning reminds us of the
threat and rescue of another baby, Jesus, born into danger when the
power of a hostile state was harnessed for evil, but could not prevent
God's plan unfolding.

The women displayed qualities of bravery, determination and fore-
sight. When Pharaoh became nervous of the mass of Hebrew slaves,
he ordered all the baby boys to be drowned at birth by the two Hebrew
midwives. But they conspired to avoid this, risking their safety,
impelled by a compassion that defied orders or fear. So Pharaoh
ordered the Egyptian soldiers to carry out his decree by drowning all
the boys in the Nile.

Next, we meet Moses' birth mother who hid him until it was
impossible to keep him secret any longer. Rather than see him killed,
she sent him out into the unknown, just as destitute women in our
history had to, and many still do in poorer countries, leaving their
children on the steps of hospitals, convents and orphanages, praying
that this fragile life may somehow prosper. We might compare the
papyrus basket that the mother prepared for Moses to the Kinder-
transport trains that brought Jewish children away from certain
danger in Hitler's Reich to an uncertain future here in Britain. At

least the mothers could cling to hope that the children had a chance of surviving.

> May the God who weeps the tears of mothers,
> protect all women who, even today,
> suffer in civil war and invasion,
> and cannot protect their children from harm.

Moses' mother didn't abandon him to his fate entirely. Desperate to know what would happen to him, she arranged for his older sister Miriam – we can imagine a sturdy but nervous six-year-old, perhaps – to stand by as he floated away. So she saw Pharaoh's daughter, a princess of the oppressive regime, rescue the baby, for 'she felt sorry for him', though she knew full well he was one of the condemned race. Miriam bravely stepped forward and offered to fetch a Hebrew wet nurse for the child – maybe her youthful initiative but, more likely, all part of the mother's plan. For of course, the nurse who came was none other than his own mother.

> Bless all women who foster, who have the courage to adopt,
> all surrogates who act out of compassion.
> May all mothers love openly, freely and with generosity.

This must have been a very risky business, but the story suggests that all the women were complicit in the deceit and eager to co-operate, putting the protection of the child before their own security, as is the eternal law of motherhood. It's really difficult not to assume that the princess knew exactly who this fortuitous nurse was. So the two women shared Moses – the natural mother for his infancy, and the princess taking him when he was older. It was then that she named him Moses because 'I drew him out of the water'.

This is a story of God working through women of very different class, race and background, all ready to thwart the oppressor. Down the ages, what women have lacked in physical strength, they have made up for by inner strength. Moses was entrusted to another, shared and so saved. The mother made the sacrifice, the sister was the intrepid go-between, and the princess open-hearted and open-minded enough to ignore the differences between them. And through the whole of the early story of Moses' life flowed the Nile, Egypt's life-giving water.

Moses was born into danger, saved by the strength of women
and carried to safety by water.
He rescued his people by parting the Red Sea
and brought water out of the desert rock to sustain them.
May God our Mother give us a share in that life-giving water,
the commitment that never runs dry,
the courage that overflows,
the love that is always replenished.
Amen.

A *discerning heart:*
the judgement of Solomon

---

1 Kings 3

> God of Wisdom, teach me the difference between right and
> wrong.
> Help me learn the truth about love.

'Ask me for whatever you want me to give you', said God to the new
king, Solomon. How trusting to issue such a blank cheque! This is like
the opening of a fairy story, when the fairy godmother or the genie
offers the hero three wishes, and we see his foolish choices end in
disaster when he learns too late how he's wasted the great chance of
a lifetime on hollow desires.

> Generous Lord, may I ask for lasting treasure in my prayers,
> treasure that will not rot, or decay or spoil.

Although a young man in his prime, Solomon acknowledged his
dependency – 'I am only a child,' he said. And yet in this was wisdom,
for it meant he asked for the most important gift of all: 'So give your
servant a discerning heart to govern your people and distinguish
between right and wrong.' In Solomon we see that true discernment
is not a matter of intellect but of judgement and empathy. When
heart and mind are truly integrated, there wisdom is found.

This Lent we've been meeting characters who only think with their
hearts, and get things horribly wrong. We met two mothers like that,
Sarah driven by jealousy to punish her rival, and Rebekah by maternal
ambition to prejudice Esau's future. Now Solomon meets another
pair of mothers, disputing who is the rightful mother of a child. This
nightmare can still happen and our newspapers report such horrors
not infrequently – babies mixed up in hospital cots, or IVF implants

into the wrong womb, or surrogacy arrangements that break down, when the two mothers fight over who has the right to bring up the child. When Solomon is asked to pronounce a particularly difficult judgement, we learn not only about his wisdom but also the difference between wise and foolish motherhood, and true and false love.

For a true mother's love will always put the child first, as we saw in the story of Moses yesterday. How many mothers, when faced with their child's suffering, haven't said, 'It should be me; let me sit the exam; let me have the operation; let me endure the heartache.' Isn't this similar to the message we received from Jesus on the cross? For this is what God actually did on Good Friday: he bore our pain through Jesus.

> Lord Jesus, we thank you for your great act of mothering,
> placing your children's lives before your own,
> as you suffered on the cross.

The foolish mother showed the extreme corrosiveness of possessiveness: 'Neither I nor you shall have him!' she declared (v. 26), urging Solomon to carry out his threat to cut the child in two. Instantly she revealed the truth: the wise mother's answer to Solomon's test was that she would rather lose her child than see it harmed.

Both women in this story were prostitutes – they were the lowest of the low, and the least to be trusted. But one of them rose above her reputation. Though neither were ascribed any value in their society, one displayed 'the wisdom of Solomon'. People can be wise regardless of their class, or education or age. They can be wise regardless of the experiences they've had in life. Most of all, they will be wise and compassionate if their heart and mind are bound together, feeling tempered by thought, and thought nourished by prayer.

> Wise God, bless my thinking.
> Just God, bless my decisions.
> Compassionate God, bless my actions.
> Amen.

Mary at the foot of the cross

———•◆•———

John 19.25–27

Mary came to the foot of the cross, drawn as by a magnet. This was the only place on earth to be; the whole universe spinning around this wasteland. There was no choice in her being there, only the necessity of a mother's love.

Suffering Jesus, bless all mothers who share their child's agony.

Mary closed her eyes at the foot of the cross, unable to bear the horror of what she saw, but compelled to be near her son while he still breathed.

Suffering Jesus, give us the courage of your mother to stay near and outstare evil.

Mary clung to the foot of the cross, refusing to let go.

Lord, help us know when it is time to let go of hope, of loved ones, of safety.

Mary stood at the foot of the cross, but only with the help of friends. Without them, she'd have had no strength to stand.

Thank you, God, for friends who keep us upright in our darkest days.

Mary remembered at the foot of the cross a happy baby, the simple shepherds, the gift of gold, the home in Nazareth, the love of Joseph.

Thank you, God, for the good times in my life; help me realize that no pain or tragedy can cancel out the experience of beauty or love.

Mary remembered at the foot of the cross Simeon's warning, the gift of myrrh, the violence of Herod, the flight to Egypt, her son's harsh words.

Suffering Jesus, help me hold in my heart the contradictions of life, and grasp the meaning of pain.

Mary prayed at the foot of the cross, begging God to act NOW. As fear grew, so did her estrangement from God; as shame and humiliation overwhelmed her, she prayed no more. As the light faded, so did all hope.

Listening God, when we're too tired to pray, too full of woe, be gentle with our despair.

Mary's heart broke at the foot of the cross, alone in the world, till she heard the words, 'Dear woman, here is your son.'

Loving Lord, do not leave us comfortless.

Mary listened at the foot of the cross, straining to hear her son's breathless words. She thought she heard him say 'forgive'.

Forgiving Jesus, help us hear your quiet words, above the clamour of our inhumanity.

Mary grieved at the foot of the cross, no consolation possible, but resolved not to hate.

Lord, give me the love and strength to reject bitterness and hatred, however hurt I am.

Mary waited at the foot of the cross, until they took her son down. When they laid him in her arms, she cradled him, like a newborn baby, her mothering come full circle. And then her tears began to fall.

Lord, give to all who mourn, mothers in particular, the healing balm of tears.

The full extent of his love

> Loving Jesus, touch me and wash me;
> wash me clean of my sin and complicity,
> wash me with your love
> till I am free to serve as you have served.

The Jesus we meet in the Gospels is the most mature, most whole, most integrated personality in history, literature or life. And because he was so secure in his identity, he had no need to put others down or diminish them. Whereas our worldly way is to divide into either/or and insist we can only be this or that, Jesus never did. Modern pop-psychology makes superficial explanations out of complex psychological studies, so that now we all wonder if we are predominately 'right brained' (intuitive) or 'left brained' (analytical), or an ambitious Type A or a laid-back Type B personality. Women and men have been encouraged to see themselves as from Venus or Mars. Yet we all know assertive women, and we all know gentle men.

Jesus defies all these categories. As much as we call him our saviour, and our teacher, he was also, in Dame Julian of Norwich's words, our true mother, 'who is all love [bearing] us into joy and endless living' (Llewelyn, *Enfolded in Love*, p. 36). In him the fullness of humanity was united into one breathing person, showing us how we could be transformed if we allowed our God-given potential to be released.

One of the stories in John's Gospel which clearly shows this mothering of Jesus comes at the Last Supper. The passage opens 'Having loved his own who were in the world, he loved them to the end' (John 13.1), and he did this by washing their feet. To us this is a very maternal action, like a mother washing a newborn with delight and amazement, or a nurse washing a frail old man who finds every movement difficult, every jolt a shock.

> Caring Jesus, bless all who care for others,
> those who care out of love, and those who care as employment;
> give them patience and kindness, and the strength to
>   continue day after day.

In our modern Anglo-Saxon society we have strict, if unwritten, codes about touching. Beyond a handshake or an artificial peck on the cheek, we only hold those we are closest to. As adults we only hug and cuddle people we love intimately. Children are much less inclined to ration touch. Perhaps that is another reason Jesus said they were first in his kingdom. Jesus never recoiled from intimacy – he bathed our feet, and let others do likewise, he gave us food, he touched the unclean. By this he set an example of Christian fellowship and witness, built on humility, intimacy and service. Jesus loved from pure impulse, without having to think or examine his motives, for it was the essence of his nature and Sonship. We, however, being trapped in our frailty, must train our awareness and pray that loving responses, gestures and words will, as we grow as Christians, become natural to us too.

> Mother Jesus, may your pulse of love beat in my heart,
> and my touch carry your compassion.

After all the nurturing Jesus did for us, he took his care to its final conclusion, picking up the cross for us and bearing our burdens. As a child grows in size, becoming heavier and heavier, he'll still run to Mum when sick, or sad or hurting, throwing his arms up in the air, certain that she'll lift him into the safety of her arms. A loving mother will clasp the child tight and carry him, however exhausted she feels. Just in this way, Jesus carried our sins through the streets of Jerusalem and nailed them to the cross of wood and shame. All the sins of history, all the sins that led up to his death, and the sins of the future, yet to be committed – how heavy were all these!

> We call that day Good Friday,
> for on that day you bore our woe,
> your love outpoured, your mercy flowing,
> you proved your love and now I know
> you love me as a mother.
> Amen.

WEEK 5: FRIENDS AND STRANGERS

When did we see you a stranger and invite you in?
(Matthew 25.38)

Go and do likewise:
the Good Samaritan

Luke 10.25–37

> Jesus our Teacher, help us find new ways
> to understand the ancient parables you taught.
> So may eternal truths and values
> speak to our generation.

It was an 'expert in the law' who asked the tricky question – some may say the trick question – 'And who is my neighbour?' The real-life answer is often bleak, responding to the obvious fact that we care more for our nearest and dearest than we do for strangers. So who are the experts in the law that we might turn to today, and what would be their answer? An evolutionary biologist might say our 'selfish genes' insist we have no stake in the future of a stranger. Social psychologists point to studies that show we'll risk hardship only if we are closely related to a victim. Philosophers debate what claims we can have on others, and try to weigh up what obligations we owe in a society where we can only know a fraction of the population personally. Politicians are keen to ration support by dividing up the 'deserving' and the 'undeserving' – yet who are we to judge? And the media delight in telling us who *isn't* our neighbour – particularly the asylum seeker and the refugee.

> Lord of the outsider, help me examine my attitudes
> to people who make me uncomfortable,
> and help me listen to their stories.

Last summer, God showed me his answer to the question in a modern version of the parable of the Good Samaritan. It wasn't a unique experience, but it was unforgettable. Our boat trip from Penzance to the Isles of Scilly began as a sheltered cruise down to Land's End where the swell gets stronger as you head into open sea. At that moment the announcement came: 'Is there a doctor of medicine on board?' A woman was very ill, and it was decided we should turn back to Penzance to meet the Royal Navy Air-Sea Rescue helicopter in calmer waters. Our ferry was compact and we felt we could almost touch the helicopter as it whirred overhead, and could see the shine on the officer's shoes as he was let down onto the tiny deck.

After much activity, the officer was winched up, gently supporting the woman strapped to a cradle-stretcher.

In Jesus' story, the man beaten on the Jericho road by robbers was taken to safety on a donkey; this woman was hoisted into the air by perfect strangers, and the donkey was now a helicopter. As the Samaritan paid with his own money for the man's care in the inn, so all of us, through our taxes, paid for the rescue – the training of the crews, the upkeep of the helicopter, and the treatment the woman would receive in hospital. It could have run into thousands of pounds.

> May we be generous because we have received;
> may we give without constraints.

As the helicopter flew away, the passengers spontaneously applauded. Why? Of course, we applauded the skill and dedication of the crews; and we applauded as a prayer to the woman – 'God speed! Get well!' But most of all we wanted to be included in all the efforts, for we recognized the basic truth that the sanctity of human life overrides all differences. The person was a complete stranger to us; we knew not whether she was a saint or a sinner, a foolish young drug-dealer or a tired old woman, yet we shared a common identity.

> Saviour Jesus, when I am wounded, rescue me,
> when I am strong, may I rescue the weak.

We turned on our way, nearly two hours late, but not one person grumbled. How well we understood: we are literally 'all in the same boat'. When Jesus asked the expert in the law who was neighbour to the beaten man, his answer was, 'The one who had mercy on him'. Mercy doesn't require proof of obligation, or balance rights and responsibilities. So the questioner learnt something no law books could teach him; and that day in the middle of the sea, we did too.

> Benevolent God, bless all who show mercy in your name,
> and all agencies who care in my name,
> in places I'll never visit, with people I'll never meet.
> Amen.

Because he loved him as himself: David and Jonathan

1 Samuel

I have told you this so that my joy may be in you
and that your joy may be complete . . .
Love each other as I have loved you.

(John 15.11, 12)

No look at friendship in the Bible would be complete without the story of David, a shepherd, and Jonathan, son of a king. It seems they 'clicked' immediately – 'Jonathan became one in spirit with David, and he loved him as himself.' Another way of describing that would be to say they were soulmates. How we all long for such a friend – someone with whom we can be totally ourselves, and who understands our every word and even our thoughts. But not all friendships are so special. Communicating between people can be like going on a train journey – to get anywhere interesting the train must cross over the points where two different lines converge. If the train glides across, it arrives in a new, interesting place. But if the points break down, the train is derailed.

Listening Jesus, may we become attentive
to the true meaning behind another's words.
Help me to read between the lines.

What are the foundation stones of friendship, apart from good listening? The initial attraction is unscientific and unpredictable, and rises above differences. But for the friendship to mature, trust must flourish. It's taken for granted in families, which is why when it's broken, as it was between the brothers Jacob and Esau, it is seen as so appalling. But between friends, trust is entirely voluntary, because friendship is not reliant on obligations or roles, but on free will.

95

David and Jonathan trusted each other with their lives. David, knowing that Saul (Jonathan's father, and once his friend, too), was turning against him, relied on Jonathan to find out how much danger he was really in. When Jonathan came to give the agreed secret signal, telling David to flee (1 Samuel 20.35), he knew Jonathan wouldn't trick him, for Jonathan had earlier made a covenant with him. Though David then was the inferior, Jonathan had privately renounced his claim to the throne as Saul's son, and promised to pass it to David. So out of their friendship, equality developed.

The story escalated to crisis and their trust was severely tested. For Jonathan, the situation was a dreadful dilemma. Whom did he owe loyalty to most of all – his friend to whom he had pledged allegiance, or his father to whom he was tied by blood and custom? How was he to decide – flip a coin, or toss a dice, or consider deep in his heart? How do we decide?

> Friend Jesus, when I am faced with conflicting loyalties
> help me reach a wise decision,
> act with honour and honesty
> and retain respect for all.

'Whatever you want me to do, I'll do for you,' Jonathan had said. This promise put him on a collision course with his father. 'Don't I know that you have sided with [David] to your own shame?' declared Saul (1 Samuel 20.30).

When Jonathan acted to save David, David thanked him not with words, but he 'bowed down before Jonathan three times, with his face to the ground' (1 Samuel 20.41), mirroring the honour Jonathan had shown him when he'd pledged his covenant. Then they kissed each other and wept.

> Eyes that meet reveal the soul,
> a smile says more than words,
> tears are a whole language of grief;
> a hand held, speaks of comfort.
> No words need ever be spoken.

David and Jonathan never met again. Jonathan's way of reconciling his honour and duty with his love was to stay with Saul and fight against the Philistines. And when news reached David of his death at the hands of the enemy, and of Saul's own death, David mourned them both. His lament, in 2 Samuel 1, 'How the mighty have fallen', grieved for both the father whose friendship had failed him and the son whose friendship never faltered, whose 'love for me was wonderful'.

> Greater love has no one than this:
> to lay down one's life for one's friends.
>
> (John 15.13)

He called her forward: four women who met Jesus

Luke 13; John 4; Luke 7; Matthew 15

Though I am an outsider, I am included,
though I am sinful, I am accepted,
though I am sick, I am healed.
Though I am a nameless stranger
God recognizes me.

I wonder if anywhere there is a stained-glass window dedicated to the many anonymous women that Jesus met and ministered to? If not, I'd like to nominate four candidates, all strangers lost in their own desert of despair without any way out, who allowed themselves to be transformed by their encounter.

The first quarter of the window would be in glass the colour of the earth – burnt umbers and sienna, the colour of soil and sand, which was all this woman, bent double for 18 years, could see. She was never able to lift her head to the indigo sky or the silver stars, or the ripe lemon trees. She had been standing on the women's side of the synagogue when Jesus spotted her, and in his compassion, he called her forward. She had never given up hope, so out she hobbled, braving the ire of the Pharisees, for this was the Sabbath. Jesus laid his hands on her and she was 'set free' in spirit and straightened in body: made whole (Luke 13.10–13).

Healing Jesus, when you call me forward, I will come;
When I am bent double, you will straighten me.

The second quarter of this masterpiece would be in the pale transparent blue of water, the water that gushes from a hillside spring, fresh and jubilant, the clear sparkling water of a natural well. At such a well Jesus met a woman of Samaria (John 4), and casually, but controversially, asked her 'Will you give me a drink?' In the course of a strange and confusing conversation, Jesus told her 'everything I've ever done'. His intuition was of God, and humans will never attain such perfect perception. But saint-like people are often recognised by their ability to penetrate another's inner being. Is it because they are able to eradicate all the interference of their own egos, so they are open to receive the signals from the other?

> You have searched me, Lord, and you know me.
> You know when I sit and when I rise;
> you perceive my thoughts from afar.
> You discern my going out and my lying down;
> you are familiar with all my ways.
>
> (Psalm 139.1–3)

Jesus won this woman's trust, and converted her, and she received the spring of eternal life. Nor did she keep her gift to herself, for she eagerly shared it with her neighbours.

These two women were approached by Jesus, but the next two subjects of our window made their own decision to seek him out. The third section would be purple, the colour of Lent, of repentance. It is the colour of the shame of the sinful woman who anointed Jesus' feet with costly perfume (Luke 7.36–50). She is shown with neck bent and hair falling over her face. Once, long before, Moses had accused his people of being 'stiff-necked', and that's a good description of the Pharisees who looked on so sternly at this woman. It is impossible to be wise and stiff-necked at the same time, for you only see one point of view that way, and in life that is never enough. The penitent can be wise: this woman who brought the alabaster jar, who stood behind Jesus weeping, and wiped his feet with her hair, could not have done that without stooping. We never hear her words, for it is her actions which beg for forgiveness, which Jesus, to the fury of the Pharisees, promised her.

> Dry my tears of guilt, Lord,
> and grant me the peace you promise.

The final picture would be in blazing oranges, the orange of fire, and protest and determination. A gentle woman, a Canaanite, was desperate for her daughter to be cured and went to Jesus (Matthew 15.21–28), only to be rebuffed because, Jesus said, she was not from Israel. But she fell at his feet – just like the sinful woman – and her bold protest, 'even the dogs eat the crumbs that fall from their master's table', opened Jesus' heart. Through this encounter, not only was the daughter cured, but the outsider and foreigner was and is forever welcomed into the Kingdom.

> Stranger God, I long to know you better.
> Affectionate God, stay close to me.
> Unknowable God, I bow before your mystery,
> Approachable God, stay by my side.
> Amen.

You have made them equal to us: the workers in the vineyard

Matthew 20.1–16

> Give, and it will be given to you. A good measure, pressed down,
> shaken together and running over, will be poured into your lap.
> For with the measure you use, it will be measured to you.
>
> (Luke 6.38)

How lovely is the sight of a vineyard, green branches stretching up a hillside, sinuous hands of succulent purple grapes waiting to be picked and turned into wine. But it must be backbreaking work, no more glamorous than strawberry picking or digging up potatoes. A whole day's toil in the vineyard would be exhausting. Yet all the men in Jesus' story wait in hope to be hired – how else could they earn a day's wage to feed the family? The landowner didn't have a regular workforce but chose from the motley group queuing to be taken on. Nor did he appear at first sight to be particularly sympathetic. 'Why have you been standing here all day long doing nothing?' he asked. How often we still hear that complaint today – 'why don't the unemployed smarten up and get a job?' We should stop and think what it is about our economic systems which prevent them, before we judge too hastily.

> Lord God of the workers, help our economies become so
> ordered
> that young and old can be employed in work that fulfils them,
> feeds their family and nourishes their dignity.

The men may have been sweaty and scruffy, but the landowner didn't dismiss them as unemployable. He didn't insist his workers project a company image. He didn't employ 'people like us', which is what, if left to our instincts, we'll always do. For our way of feeling safe with strangers is to relate with 'people like us', and shun those who are different.

The workers who thought they were favoured, who'd done everything right and got there early, were horrified when they found that the late-comers were paid the same. 'You have made them equal to us', they complained. Therein lay their real anger – they responded with the instinct common to human nature that not only categorizes, but puts people into preferred hierarchies. And it's no surprise that when we do this we put our needs, rights and deserts higher than the stranger's. How easy it is to see ourselves as deserving, how tempting to say the other is undeserving. But Jesus said: They are equal to you. 'So the last will be first, and the first will be last': Jesus rips up our orderly lists and jumbles us all together.

> When you appeal to me on the basis of love,
> may I step back from my place as first in the queue
> and embrace the other as equal.

If we continually employ 'people like us', we discriminate against the outsider – the black, the gay, the dyslexic. Modern recruitment procedures are devised precisely to inhibit our natural, closed instincts. God is definitely an 'Equal Opportunity Employer'. He wants all to have a chance to prove 'you have made them equal to us'. God is willing to use everyone and anyone for his purposes.

Isn't that what Jesus did when he collected his group of disciples around him? They came from all walks of life and he bound them together through loyalty to himself and to a common purpose. In this way a group of strangers became a group of disciples. In the same way, each contributing what we can, we can become members of the Body of Christ – a new community formed of surprising relationships.

> Early in the morning, Lord, come and find me.
> At midday, I will be waiting.
> Even at the eleventh hour, you still welcome me,
> for it is never too late to become your disciple.
> Amen.

Woe to you, you hypocrites: Philemon's reply

———◆•◆———

Philemon

Jesus, it is our hypocrisy you most deplore.
May I never be scornful of others,
or shut the door of the Kingdom in another person's face.
(cf. Matthew 23.13)

Most Reverend Paul,

We are so distressed to hear you are still in prison, and will pray for your release, as will Apphia and Archippus, and I will insist the whole household does too; I won't let anyone shirk this duty.

And of course, when the glad day arrives and you are set free, I would count it an honour for so great a man as you to stay in my humble home.

As for the small matter you raise in your letter, there are some difficulties in what you ask. Once Onesimus ran away, I replaced him quite quickly. My neighbour had a young slave that he no longer required and he recommended him to me as a hard worker, so I took him on for a trial period. He's proved excellent, he's never sleepy in the morning, is strong in muscle and quick in wit. So I would feel it unfair to dismiss him, and I really don't need an extra pair of hands or mouth to feed.

Of course, all the other slaves know of Onesimus' absconding, and the unfortunate circumstances, and I fear it would be a very bad judgement to have him back. I would lose respect, and discipline would collapse, I'm sure.

Much as I personally may be able to forgive him in time, I'm certain my wife could not; after all, it was her brooch he took and she was very fond of it – it was her grandmother's. She wept copious tears at its loss. I do feel that in this life we must suffer the consequences of our actions, surely? I gave him one chance, treated him well, and look how he repaid me. How many more chances can he expect?

I know what a quick thinker you are, but I confess I found your sentence a bit jumbled, the one that starts 'Perhaps the reason he was separated from you . . .' for I was very surprised by the way you seem to suggest he return not as a slave at all, but as a – *brother*? Did you really mean that or was it the scribe's bad handwriting? I can't really understand how you would expect that – I already have two brothers, very dear to me, but they have their own households, and I wouldn't expect them to share my home, so what would I do with Onesimus? I really couldn't face him strutting around as if he was my equal; that would never do. Society needs some rules, Paul, or everything would collapse. Don't you agree?

No, no, it's all too complicated, I'm afraid. Of course I wish him well, and hope it works out for him. But another thing, Paul, if you don't mind me saying so, don't you think you're being a little naïve? How do you know he's to be trusted? Just because you had such an amazing transformation, you think others can too, but you're the exception that proves the rule; leopards rarely change their spots.

To bring you up to date with the church here, we've begun planning the new worship room and have a contractor who'll do it for a good price and not cheat us, as that last scoundrel did. I think he'd heard our Lord's story, the one about the workers in the vineyard who get paid a full day's wage for only one hour's work, and thought Jesus meant it to be taken literally!

I send you my greetings and consolation while you are in prison, and pray that the kingdom will come one day soon.

Yours respectfully,

Philemon

> Brother Jesus, give me insight into my motives,
> so that I know what it is I am defending,
> what it is I am ignoring,
> and what I am guarding myself against today.
> Amen.

Betrayed by a word, betrayed with a kiss: Judas and Jesus

Matthew 26, 27

God our Judge, none of us sees clearly the consequences
  of our actions:
when we know we've made a wrong decision,
give us strength to seek reconciliation.

We only meet Judas at the end of the Gospels, at his moment of supreme crisis, the time when he is faced with a dreadful choice. Damned by this one action, his reputation is beyond rescue. This is the point of his fateful decision. What has gone before to form his character is irrelevant to the Gospel writers. Yet he was one of the Twelve. He was Jesus' friend and companion. The word companion derives from the 'one who breaks bread with another'. It denotes a sharing and an equality. In traditional societies, you didn't eat with your lord. A companion is also someone who travels with you, who walks alongside, who jokes, enjoys the view, and shares the hardship. Companions complement each other. All these, Judas had been to Jesus. Try to imagine their good times together.

Judas' occasional furrowed brow or moody withdrawal would have been nothing to be too concerned about. Jesus was used to his disciples disappointing him. Peter did, several times, James and John did at least once, when they vied for precedence in the kingdom. But did Judas ever 'have it out' with Jesus? If, instead of bottling up his inner conflicts, till his judgement become wildly distorted and his moral compass shattered, he had had the sense to talk to Jesus, things might have turned out differently.

Lord, when through confusion, envy or ambition
I wander into the desert of sin,
help me discern the path to safety.

The final, tragic end to Judas' story – his remorse when Jesus is condemned, his desperate attempt to put things right, are not unique. Just before we learn of Judas' suicide, we read of Peter's great betrayal: 'I don't know the man!' he said to the servant who challenged him (Matthew 26.72). Both in the end confessed, but Judas' tragedy was that Jesus was not there to hear the confession. Peter became a saint, while Judas becomes the embodiment of evil, and a noun for all who betray a friend. So close is the difference between exile and the reconciliation, it almost seems unfair.

What if Judas hadn't despaired and killed himself, but gone instead to the foot of the cross and begged forgiveness of Jesus? Do we honestly think Jesus would have denied him?

> 'Father, forgive them, for they do not know what they are
>   doing' –
> you prayed in your agony, leaving no one outside your
>   embrace,
> not even me.

Judas' betrayal might have been for silver, or because he was disillusioned by Jesus' lack of a plan. It could have been impatience for the revolution, or anger when Jesus had condoned the woman's waste of precious oil, or fear that Jesus would bring them all down with him. We never know another's motives. We should cease our speculation, and leave it between Judas and Jesus themselves. 'Since there is much more than we know going on in what is going on, when things go wrong, have gone wrong, however carefully we sift the evidence, we shall never arrive at that place of accusing light where we know who is to blame and who is not to blame' (J. N. Ward, *Friday Afternoon*, p. 18).

> Forgiving God, I only dare judge myself.
> Shine your light on my secret fears.

As we approach Holy Week, let us reflect on all the lesser betrayals we commit on an almost daily basis, without even noticing or defining them as such.

Whenever we let someone down
we let ourselves down too.
And when we let ourselves down
we diminish ourselves in God's eyes;
but never in his love.
Amen.

In two minds:
Joseph of Arimathea

―・●・―

John 19.38–42

> Lord, when my thoughts are in turmoil,
> help me look calmly and think clearly,
> and have the courage to change my mind.

When our hearts say one thing, but our mind tells us another; when our upbringing insists on one point of view but our conscience points us in another direction; when our thoughts keep us awake at night, it's probably because we're 'in two minds' about some issue or another. Often it's an old mindset that we know we must shed, as a snake sheds its skin, making way for new growth, and different behaviour.

Joseph of Arimathea went through just this upheaval in the last week of Jesus' life. He straddled two worlds – the Jewish priestly hierarchy and the fresh radical community of the man Jesus. For a while he tried sitting on the fence, in fear of ridicule and loss of status if he came out publicly for Jesus. He was understandably anxious and insecure about the future. As a prominent member of the Council which had manoeuvred for Jesus' death, he had argued against it, but kept secret that he was in fact a disciple of the condemned man (John 19.38). Sometimes the time to act or speak out is given us just once, and if the opportunity is lost, we must live with the consequences for ever. Perhaps Joseph lived the rest of his life regretting that he hadn't argued harder or sooner to save Jesus.

> When I'm faced with a choice between acting honourably
> or saving my reputation, help me take the hard decision.

Joseph wasn't in the inner circle of disciples, and certainly wasn't one of the Twelve. He was one of the larger group who carried on with their own lives but followed Jesus when they could. He certainly wasn't with him at the Last Supper. Would he have presumed to call himself a friend of Jesus? Probably not; friend and disciple are not interchangeable terms. The key disciples did relate to Jesus with a degree of ease and equality that might earn the title friend. But in Gethsemane, even these men didn't act as true friends should.

> Though my eyes are heavy and I need to rest,
> help me keep watch with my friend in need.

(You may want to name a particular person here . . .)

Who was it that did behave as closest friend to Jesus after his death? Joseph of Arimathea did not run away with the others. He displayed four signs of being a friend: he was *determined* when he went 'boldly' to Pilate to beg for Jesus' body; he was *generous* when he gave his own tomb for the burial; he was *practical* in making all the arrangements, and *intimate* in wrapping Jesus in the linen before laying him to rest – not a duty a prominent man would expect to perform, but he didn't flinch from touching the wounds or fear contamination through contact with a dead body. From being marginal – would Jesus even have known him by name? – he became the closest companion Jesus had. No longer in two minds, Joseph's understanding was entirely focused on his dead Master and so he grew in stature throughout this dreadful experience. His compassion had been awoken by the suffering of Jesus, and he proved a depth of character in the service he gave. He truly earned himself the right to call himself a friend of Jesus.

> Crucified Jesus, unite my scattered thoughts
> and untangle my confused ideas;
> help me direct all my attention to you
> and be known as your friend.
> Amen.

WEEK 6: THE POWERFUL (HOLY WEEK)

He has brought down rulers from their thrones
but has lifted up the humble.
(Luke 1.52, the Song of Mary)

Palm Sunday:
your King comes to you

────── ◆◆◆ ──────

Matthew 21.1–11

Lord of the universe, you alone are the true ruler of all.
Direct our journeying till we find the way
to bring in the reign of the Servant King.

The confrontation had been building up for months. Through all those
healings on the Sabbath, and consorting with sinners, and insulting
the Pharisees, Jesus challenged false authority and foolish hierarchies.
The people loved him for his boldness and his honesty. Now Jesus
had arrived in Jerusalem, surely things would change? He just had
to say the word. And so they called out 'Hosanna to the Son of
David!'

To them, Jesus was as brave as David, and they hoped he'd be as
triumphant too. David had been their all-time greatest king, the model
every king was compared with, and the prototype hero. So how did
Jesus compare to him; in what way was he the Son of David? Both
David and Jesus started from the same place – the rock of their
reliance on God.

Yours, LORD, is the greatness and the power
and the glory and the majesty and the splendour,
for everything in heaven and earth is yours.
Yours, LORD, is the kingdom; you are exalted as head over all.

(1 Chronicles 29.11, 12)

In this, David's prayer, we see a glimpse of the Lord's Prayer. David
had gone on, in God's name, to win battles and defeat enemies. If
Jesus was a king, he wouldn't win victories with armies and soldiers.
His weapons were words, and his strategy was love, and his objective

was the elevation of the meek. There'd been hints all along, especially in the Sermon on the Mount – 'How blest are those of a gentle spirit; they shall have the earth for their possession' (Matthew 5.5 NEB). Jesus gave an even bigger clue when he arrived through the gate: 'Your king comes to you,/gentle and riding on a donkey' (Matthew 21.5 quoting Zechariah 9.9). A mule is not a war horse. Jesus was determined to overturn ancient assumptions along with the tables in the Temple. He invoked kingship only to reject it; if he was a king, his power was disguised as weakness. Here, he parted company with his illustrious ancestor David.

> Servant King, for whom the purpose of power is to
>   give it away,
> may we never use power to dominate others
> or protect our own interests,
> but always to release the oppressed.

Jesus did not waste much breath berating governments or rulers or empires. He didn't encourage us to look for others to blame, but always shone a light on our own attitudes, challenging each of us to look inwards at the ways we abuse our own authority. For we do all wield power of some sort, and many of us are masters and mistresses at manipulating it in very subtle ways. Think about the parent who shouts at a toddler in the supermarket and makes stupid threats they can't possibly carry out; or the carer in charge of the incontinent elderly, who deliberately delays attending to them, or the petty official who refuses to act with flexibility or humanity. And the effect of all this power play is to destroy, and not to build up, relationships. Think how you feel after such an encounter.

> Holy Trinity, you joyfully partner power with each other.
> Teach us that power comes from unity
> and blessings flow from co-operation.

This week our concerns are with relationships governed by public power structures. When Jesus had set out on his ministry, he'd faced the temptations in the desert. There he had refused to pick up the mantle of worldly authority, and at that moment in effect he rejected the chance of becoming a second David. Women seemed to understand the difference instinctively – his mother Mary knew that God's way was to lift up the humble.

Once Jesus began the agonizing walk along the Via Dolorosa, he left behind all pretensions of authority, and knew that following this road, step by step, was the only way he could exercise his power. He was back with the ordinary people he'd come to serve – the weary soldiers, the barren women, the harassed shopkeepers and labourers. He left behind the Temple – God was no more to be found there than on the battlefield. His only weapon was submission to the cross.

> King of peace, release us from conflict,
> Servant King, give us strength
> to leave behind the wilderness
> and walk through sacrifice to transformation.
> Amen.

The fifth kingdom

Daniel 2; Matthew 5

God of history, you control the times and the seasons,
you set up kings and depose them.
Teach our leaders the transience of power
and remind them they are not infallible.

If you've ever walked around the British Museum, you'll have seen the giant statues of the kings, emperors and pharaohs of earlier civilizations, looming like giants at the end of a gallery, towering over everything and dwarfing all the spectators. Their very size was an attempt to stamp awe and fear in their subjects, and to maintain power over the beholder even after death. But we know they are now in the side room of history, relegated to a gallery of failed empires. As Percy Bysshe Shelley wrote, at the end of his poem 'Ozymandias', 'Round the decay/ Of that colossal wreck, boundless and bare/The lone and level sands stretch far away.' So we find ourselves back in yet another wilderness.

You don't have to be a historian to know that similar follies continue today. The twentieth century was a time of violence, war and revolution. Tsarist Russia fell first; then Germany – twice, and the British Empire faded away. Hopes of peace were dashed by a cold war which arose between Soviet Russia and the new great power, the USA. Now China is rivalling America as the new 'super' power.

God of peace, rescue all casualties of violent political upheaval.
Give a new future to those who exist in refugee camps,
and may the orphans of war know your love.

The prophet Daniel wouldn't have been a bit surprised. He predicted such upheavals years before the birth of Jesus. He knew the Medes and Persians, the Babylonians and the Greeks would all perish. Nebuchadnezzar's crown did not rest easy on his head – hence his troubled dreams. He had a vision of an 'enormous dazzling statue, awesome in appearance' (Daniel 2.31) – his head of gold, his chest of silver, belly of bronze, legs of iron and feet of clay. Daniel knew this hybrid monster was the personification of all the worst empires of his world, and knew that the statue would crumble to dust.

There is a better way, but not one to be inaugurated by any earthly emperor. This is the way set out for us very clearly in the list of blessings called the Beatitudes. Some of them are quiet, almost passive, and relate to our 'being', not our doing: we must be meek, poor in spirit, pure in heart. Without these qualities in our heart, we will not become actively merciful, or search with passion for righteousness (that unique combination of justice and mercy), or withstand the persecution this quest is bound to excite. We usually think of these blessings as being personal qualities to be prayed for as a guide to deepening our faith. But unless we require them of people with power, the dislocation of this world will never be healed. They should be foundational to the behaviour of any leader.

If in one moment on earth, in every time zone, from the rising sun in Tokyo to the sunset in San Francisco, each one of us aligned ourselves utterly to God's will, there would be a flash of insight and an explosion of love. This would be the beginning of Daniel's 'fifth kingdom', a kingdom of peace on earth and good will to all. At present we are like a broken engine, with our cogs rusty and wheels lacking synchronization, all grinding against each other. In the fifth kingdom everything will be oiled by God's love and achieve perfect harmony.

We've seen glimpses of the possibility in the great leaders of the twentieth century – they weren't all bad. We've seen the inspiration of Martin Luther King, the peacefulness of Gandhi, the generosity of Mandela, the joy of Archbishop Tutu, the eloquence of Churchill, and the faithfulness of Queen Elizabeth II. But no mortal man or woman has ever been able to combine all these qualities and virtues. Jesus alone does that.

> God our ruler, you offer wisdom to the discerning:
> reveal your purposes to our governments,
> and bring in your eternal kingdom built on love,
> through your Son, Jesus Christ our Lord.
> Amen.

Among you stands one you do not know: John the Baptist

John 1.1–32

God of the prophets, we give thanks for John the Baptist,
for his potency, his energy, and his willingness to take
second place.

It's happened to all of us – we go to a talk to hear a famous writer, and mistake him for the caretaker, or go to a party and don't recognize our host, or arrive at a meeting and don't realize who is the boss. We have such fixed ideas of what a good leader should look like – tall, dressed in a smart suit, sporting an expensive watch and gripping a leather briefcase (and probably male). So imagine what it would have been like for the Jewish leadership when the wild prophet John declared, 'Among you stands one you do not know' (John 1.26). They glanced around nervously, staring first at this person and then the next, trying to figure out who he was talking about.

Jesus, open my eyes to the surprise
of meeting you; help me look beneath appearances
and recognize you in unlikely people.

The prophet John is a character we overlook far too much. Both the Gospels of Mark and John actually start with the Baptist, not with Jesus, and it seems it was touch and go which one would dominate the story. We know how it ends, but at the time, the leaders of the Jews did not. The fact that Jesus' story overtook John's was partly because of John's own insistence: 'He must become greater; I must become less' (John 3.30). How rare for anyone to relinquish control! John's whole ministry was one of surprises and reversals. John prophesied Jesus, but Jesus submitted to John, being baptized by him

117

because 'it is proper for us to do this to fulfil all righteousness' (Matthew 3.15). Both John and Jesus test us and challenge our assumptions about the meaning of greatness and dominance: 'The one who is least in the kingdom of God is greater than he,' Jesus says of John (Luke 7.28). This is not a criticism, it is a statement spoken in love. John agrees wholeheartedly – 'He is the one who comes after me, the straps of whose sandals I am not worthy to untie' (John 1. 27).

However unalike these two cousins were – John the ranting, dour prophet, Jesus the joyful rule-breaker—they both insisted that their most important teaching, repeated again and again, was 'For it is the one who is least among you all who is the greatest' (Luke 9.46–48). But we still don't 'get it'.

> Jesus, you took a little child and welcomed her.
> May I welcome you in the weak
> and never seek preference in your kingdom.

Herod certainly didn't 'get it' either. He didn't get it about his own position – bloated by luxury, puffed up by pride, and blinded by a deceitful family, 'humble' wasn't in his vocabulary. His powers of insight had long since been choked by the weeds of corruption. And yet he was strangely drawn to John: 'he was greatly puzzled, yet he liked to listen to him', (Mark 6.20). If only he'd listened to his inner voice instead of Salome. Stuck in the tunnel vision of his tyranny, unbending about his superiority, then titillated by Salome's dance, he would rather behead John than be shown up in front of his dinner guests!

No one would have been surprised then, and no one should be surprised now. Both the towering figures of the Gospel had their lives cut short by quasi-judicial killings. Violence is such an easy solution for a tyrant. But neither John nor Jesus were weak victims, for the power of truth lay in their hands, not Herod's, and that truth still reverberates down the centuries. Now they really are the greatest, and Herod a mere footnote.

> Lord Jesus, we exalt you.
> Help us share in your humility
> and grasp the great reversal
> your kingdom has established.
> Amen.

How long will you refuse to humble yourself? Moses and Pharaoh

————•◆•————

Exodus 7—14

> Lord God, keep me from obstinacy.
> May I always act with integrity
> and learn humility.

Moses was a murderer, who became an outcast, and then a shepherd. When he returned to his people there was no pomp, procession or entourage. Little wonder that Pharaoh was blind to his position of leadership. He didn't recognize that Moses' authority came from his deep spiritual closeness to God.

Pharaoh was the sort of leader who took more notice of external trappings than inner strength and he mistook intransigence for firm leadership. 'How long will you refuse to humble yourself?', Moses asked him. Can a leader ever dare to be humble? Pharaoh is a classic example of a person who believes he's strong when really he's surviving 'by caprice' like T. S. Eliot's 'weak man' in *Murder in the Cathedral*, p. 196.

Before we reject the story of Pharaoh's obstinacy as absurd, we should examine ourselves for the times we dismiss the evidence that's before our eyes, and cling to what suits us, because it fits in with our prejudices. A discerning heart must have the courage to interrogate itself beneath the surface.

> Lord, prompt me to recognize the times
> I ignore the lessons of reality.

On a national and international scale, this is all too evident. Leaders trust in the strength of force and are seduced through vanity and arrogance into a belief in their omnipotence, determined to ignore that they are living in a changed world.

Pharaoh's other big mistake was his short-term memory. He wanted the bad to go away and made any number of promises to get rid of the frogs, the gnats, the flies and the boils that Moses inflicted on his nation. But as soon as each crisis passed, he slipped back into false reliance on his supremacy. He's like someone with a hangover who vows 'I won't touch another drop again', or a gambler who keeps on losing but is convinced that with one more try he'll come up trumps. Temptation reasserts itself in a blasé assurance of invincibility.

Pharaoh's heart was hardened, we're told, which means he closed down his reflective self. He would not listen and could not learn. Even when he began to make concessions, he quickly reneged when the danger passed. He tried to enter negotiations with Moses – I'll let you stay and worship here; OK but don't go too far; well, just the men then; the men and the women, but not the livestock. He said one thing and meant the opposite.

> Righteous Lord, may I always mean what I say,
> and never go back on a promise.
> May I always be known as someone who keeps my word.

Eventually Pharaoh declared 'I have sinned', but yet again he backed out because he didn't truly believe this in his heart. Change must be internal, not superficial. When we really need to learn something well, we repeat it again and again until we've learnt it 'off by heart', which means it's absorbed into our very being. That is why Moses and Aaron had to persist. Like a parent who declares 'How many times have I warned you?', in the end they had to resort to punishment. The tragedy of the death of Egypt's firstborn was brought about by Pharaoh's obduracy and foolishness.

Pharaoh never did learn that the true purpose of power was the safety and security of his people. He didn't put their welfare before his own pride. The good leader always puts others first:

> Whoever wants to become great among you must be your
>   servant,
> and whoever wants to be first must be slave of all.
> For even the Son of Man did not come to be served,
> but to serve, and to give his life as a ransom for many.
>   (Mark 10.43–45)

Maundy Thursday:
I am innocent of this man's blood

———•◦•———

Luke 22.66—23.25

An inch is the gap between right and wrong,
between the cool of the house and the dazzling sun.
One step only out into the glare
the door slams quickly, you must leave there.
Forced to choose either left or right,
round the corner, out of sight.

Every decision we ever make is a risk, yet how reluctant so many of us
are to take one. There is a great difference between all the thinking that
leads up to a decision, and the moment when you sign on the dotted
line and commit yourself – to a new job, a new house, a marriage –
knowing you are moving into uncharted territory. A decision made
in a moment can last a lifetime. At Jesus' birth there were three
leaders revered for their wisdom who made the momentous decision
to search for him. From the wisdom of these men came their journey;
from their generosity came their gifts; from their humility came their
worship. At the end of Jesus' life it's his turn to visit, or rather, be
dragged, to three more leaders – Caiaphas, Herod and Pilate. Three
men shared the decision whether Jesus lived or died, three men who
laboured to do the right thing by their masters, for even the power-
ful have masters. They wriggled like fish in the deep end of political
expediency, furtively manoeuvring themselves away from the wave of
Caesar's blame, out of the snap of the big shark's jaw. All three lacked
the wisdom to take the hard decision and whatever insight they had
was blotted out by fear, like clouds covering the sun.

We can't distinguish who carried the most blame, nor try to judge.
Caiaphas ostensibly acted for the protection of his people, believing

it wise to sacrifice one troublemaker for the security of the status quo. A moral maze indeed – how does one balance the right of an individual against the benefit of many?

> Lord, when we seek the common good
> stop us pretending that the ends always justify the means.

Herod's involvement was limited, and once he discovered Jesus wasn't an all-singing, all-dancing miracle worker, he lost interest, and sent him back to Pilate. It is Pilate who struggled longer and harder to square the circle. All power involves compromise, politics being the art of the possible. In the end, circumstances forced Pilate into such a tight corner that he only had one way out, though in the Gospel accounts we sense his deep reluctance.

> For every life and every act
> Consequence of good and evil can be shown.
> And as in time results of many deeds are blended
> So good and evil in the end become confounded.
>
> (T. S. Eliot, *Murder in the Cathedral*, p. 59)

Ponder these words, and let them speak to you, and your life story.

There is another character in this story who holds great power, and that is the crowd. We see it still today, in demonstrations and protests; we see it too in the influence of our press and media which can act as a mass rabble-rouser. We see the same fickleness in the crowd who switched sides from Palm Sunday to Good Friday.

> Lord, may our press act with wisdom and restraint.
> May they use their power for the good of all
> and never crucify the innocent.

So we can't wash our hands in this calamity. Everyone is compromised and contaminated and their reasons obscured by self-deceit. Only one person is wholly innocent, and that is Jesus, whose behaviour bears scrutiny under every light and from every angle. And the dreadful irony is that those who condemned him knew that too.

The powerful (Holy Week)

Jesus, you were accused: when I act like Caiaphas
and put expediency above principle, have mercy.
Jesus, you were arrested: when I am Herod
and refuse to get involved, have mercy.
Jesus, you were condemned: when I am Pilate
and wash my hands of my responsibilities, have mercy.
Jesus, you were executed: when I am the crowd
and am prepared to crucify you, have mercy.
Amen.

Good Friday: several excuses for not following Jesus to the cross

I was too busy – it had been a horrendous week. By Friday I'm always exhausted. I had the shopping to do before everything shut for Sabbath.

Everyone deserves a bit of time to themselves, don't they?

I did think about him.

> Father, forgive my laziness and sloth.
> Forgive me when I am so half-hearted and selfish.

I forgot the time. I really intended to go when James had phoned to say the trial had taken a turn for the worse. I meant to go down to the courthouse to hear the verdict. But then I started cleaning the windows – a sudden shaft of sun showed up how dirty they were. I couldn't see through them.

Then the church clock struck three and I reckoned it was too late.

> Father, forgive me for not understanding that I use my
> busyness as an excuse.
> Or is it a way of showing where my real priorities lie?

Friends were coming to supper, you see. It would have been rude to put them off. No one could have guessed things would have reached such a pitch so soon. When we planned it, Jesus was still in the suburbs, he hadn't got the authorities up in arms against him, and everyone was pleased that he was healing so many people.

> Father, forgive the times I put pleasure before prayer;
> all the times the things of the world outweigh the
> importance of your kingdom.

Then, I don't like crowds, they always bother me. Maybe it's because I'm so small, it means I can't see over people's heads, I feel hemmed in; it doesn't take much to make me feel threatened.

Father, forgive me when I use fear as an excuse not to act.

Plus, you don't know who you might be mixing with. You go on demonstrations and before you know it, you're next to a Trotskyite or someone from the BNP. On the other hand, I might have been recognized as one of his supporters. What good would it do now, to be implicated? The cause is lost, we're in a mess, best shrink back into the shadows. I can go on trying to live by his teaching.

Father, forgive me when I refuse to get my hands dirty in the cause
  of righteousness,
because I worry what others might think of me.

Anyway, there were so many there, I couldn't make a difference, I wouldn't be missed. Jesus couldn't have known if I was there or not, so how could it have mattered?
  It would have turned out the same.

Father, forgive me when I let other people stand up for my
  beliefs.
Help me realize that making a difference must always start
  with me.

Seriously, I couldn't bear to see him suffer. It would have been horrible to watch that agony, like gawping at a horror film. It would have broken my heart to see the pain on his face.

Jesus, forgive my lack of compassion;
my refusal to share the weight of your cross,
the way I always run away from suffering.

Of course, in a way, he brought it on himself. He did rather provoke them. Was there any need to go to such extremes? All his love talk was fine; if only he hadn't taken on the leaders and priests.
  Why break so many rules? Why claim he's God or something?

Jesus, forgive me when I doubt you.
Forgive my lack of faith.

You know, I never really thought he could live up to what he promised. I'm disappointed, I put such hope in him, but there it is. How could one person ever hope to penetrate the hate and power of this world?

> Jesus, forgive my narrow vision,
> my inability to see the kingdom and live in your hope.
> Forgive me when I abandon your gospel.

And anyway, it was raining.

Holy Saturday: the empty room

The room had been empty since Thursday night, when Jesus, desperate for air, had left to be with God on the open hillside. The door slammed shut behind them, with the thud of a hammer's blow. They'd left behind the remnants of the meal – wine spilt on the table, crumbs still scattered about, and by midnight, the candle wax had dripped, like tears down a woman's face. No one came to clear away on Friday, all distracted by the commotion in the city. Sometime that afternoon, the table had shaken, the plates trembled and a cup rolled onto the floor and smashed in two.

All Saturday the room stayed unattended. It was the Sabbath; no chores could be done. The door remained firmly shut, the air grew stale and the shutters let in no light.

God of light, rescue those who live in darkness,
whose sight is blurred by sorrow,
whose vision is lost through pain or contrition.

We should not look back on Holy Saturday with hindsight – it is not the day when the world held its breath. It is the day when all hope was destroyed and all relationships shattered. The disciples had fled at Gethsemane. From now onwards they would exist but would not truly live. Some gathered together for safety, but they were not waiting for anything. Others scattered further afield, like stragglers from a defeated army, crushed and disheartened.

God of hope, rescue all who have lost hope
who have given up on life ever coming right again.

Jesus was dead; it rhymes with fled and dread. No solace was to be found that day. It was a day of no thing – nothing – of emptiness and exhaustion. There was no sound of laughter; no touch of love, for the room was empty of words or of God – all that was shut up in the stifling tomb.

> God of healing, bless all who cannot be healed,
> those born with severe impairments,
> who suffer mental anguish or physical pain.

Imagine a world devoid of any friendship or affection; no one knowing who they can trust, for even their closest friends have proved themselves capable of betrayal.

> God of relationships, Three-in-One, we pray for
>   people who endure
> brokenness and betrayal,
> who are friendless or abandoned.

The disciples were frightened, too. They feared they'd be next to be dragged off to Caiaphas or to Pilate, to be accused and condemned, swept up and imprisoned, the key thrown away, just to make sure there were no further disturbances.

> God of freedom, rescue all who will spend today,
> tomorrow and the next day, in prison cells.
> Bless all those who are unjustly held hostage,
>   deprived of their freedom.

The disciples mourned their leader, their teacher, their brother and rabbi. He had been everything to them and, without him, they were nothing. If Jesus was dead, they might as well be too.

> Giver of life, bless all those who are close to death,
> and all those who have died in the last year.
> And here I remember by name ———
> and all who still grieve their loss.

WEEK 7: RELATIONSHIP RESTORED (EASTER WEEK)

————◆◆◆————

I have seen the Lord!
(John 20.18)

Easter Sunday:
woman, why are you crying?

John 20.11–18

> When all I hear is silence,
> and my eyes are blinded by tears,
> when your love is only a memory,
> you call me into the future.

Mary came with no expectations. Today would be as desolate as yesterday. Still there was the emptiness in her heart to match the blankness of the dawn. The sun would bring no illumination – if it even rose. The day ahead was to be endured, not lived. When she found the body missing, she was desperate, not encouraged. The world just kept getting more unfathomable. Without even his wounded body to tend, Jesus was utterly lost to her. She stood to one side, weeping. Often in grief, we weep not just for the lost loved one, but also for ourselves, for our lives are utterly changed, all our expectations and sense of security torn up and flung to the howling winds.

> Lord Jesus, fulfil your promises:
> uphold me through the wilderness of abandonment,
> do not forsake me in death,
> and bring me through tragedy to a new hope.

Still she lingered; where else did she have to go? Jesus was not there, wrapped in the linen. He was not one of the angels that asked her 'why are you weeping?' He was not in the warmth of the sun that was just beginning to penetrate her bones. Her sight was obscured by tears, and her understanding by despair until she was suddenly granted 'the Spirit of wisdom and revelation' and the eyes of her heart were enlightened 'in order that you may know the hope to which he has called you' as Paul prayed in Ephesians 1.15–23.

Another word we use to describe a wise person is to say they are 'perceptive', with an inner eye that can penetrate truths hidden by events, words or body language. So often in our inner turmoil and concentration on our pain we fail to see anything properly. We see what *isn't* there, just as Mary mistook the gardener, only seeing what she expected to see. Often it is not our abilities that limit us, but our own small horizons. Nor do we see what *is* there – Jesus standing right in front of us, 'disguised as our lives', in Paula D'Arcy's much quoted phrase.

Then Mary heard the Lord in the whisper of her name.

> Without a name, we have no intimacy;
> with our name known, we have relationship.
> Risen Jesus, may I meet you in simplicity,
> in quietness and gentleness.

The only power Mary had was her steadfast faithfulness – so faithful, that all four Gospels acknowledge her primacy. It wasn't that she was unflinching – there is no virtue in that, indeed her power lay in her refusal to avoid suffering; the key to her perceptiveness was her persistence in gazing at the cross, and her dedication in coming to the tomb. She displayed all the hallmarks of the Beatitudes – she was poor in spirit, she was meek, she was in need of comfort, and these were the qualities that opened her up to God's presence, and lit her up 'like a city on a hill', bright enough to shine on all about her (cf. Matthew 5.14). So God mended her broken heart and sent her out into the world. And we are all commanded to continue with her bold claim: 'I have seen the Lord!' (John 20.18).

> Risen Lord, you surprise me by your presence.
> Bless me with the tenacity of Mary,
> speak your words into my heart
> and rise in my life today.
> Amen.

Come and have breakfast

John 21.1–14

> Risen Jesus, you come to meet us uninvited,
> and help us in apparent failure:
> come and meet us where we are.

Does it matter that the resurrection appearance of Jesus at the beach seems to be based on the earlier story of Jesus' first meeting with the fishermen, right back at the beginning of his ministry, when he called them to become fishers of men? (Luke 5.4–11). Here in John it is much developed and becomes not only a resurrection appearance, but a eucharistic meal – of sorts! Let's leave it to the scholars to debate how the stories are connected, for the important point here is that they are both stories about resurrection, because, in both, people are altered beyond recognition, turned around and re-energized. In Luke's account, ordinary fishermen become disciples; in John, frightened disciples are revived. In both, Jesus is there in the mess – 'that night they caught nothing'. Uninvited, unbidden, Jesus appeared.

> Risen Jesus, you bring abundance out of scarcity,
> and turn our lack into plenty.
> Preside at all the meals we share,
> prepare a feast for all in famine;
> come and feed us where we are.

The love of Jesus is shown in such particular ways. Here he is with the BBQ, having prepared everything in advance. There's a fire of burning coals and he's brought fresh bread. He nourishes his friends with food and lavishes them with love. He meets them in their daily struggle and values them as ordinary fishermen. He doesn't dismiss their activities, rather he affirms their sense of identity. Nor does he withhold his love until they are successful.

> Risen Jesus, you accept and support us in all our endeavours.
> Come and love us where we are.

It is only after Jesus has welcomed, sustained and affirmed us, that we are released to achieve in his name. It is Jesus who directed the disciples, 'Throw your net to the right side of the boat' and there were the fish – an enormous hoard which by rights should have torn the nets. But it is Jesus' will that all should be 'caught' for his salvation.

> Risen Jesus, give us wisdom not to strike out on our own
>   adventures,
> but to wait for you to direct us.
> When we hear your guiding voice,
> we will serve you where we are.

What made the disciple whom Jesus loved recognize the Lord? Had the boat drifted nearer the shore so that he could make out the familiar features as the grey light dawned? Or was it the timbre of Jesus' voice calling 'Friends'? Or was it the experience of being welcomed and gifted – of being saved – which was so consistent with their earlier relationship with him that he realized it could only be Jesus who had brought about this remarkable miracle?

The miracle was not only the hoard of fish itself. The more important miracle took place in their hearts, in the stunned insight: 'It is the Lord!' Accepted, sustained and affirmed through God's grace, the disciples were invigorated and enabled to see beyond the uncertainty of the dawn, into the clear noon of resurrection.

> Risen Jesus, you give us confidence
> to go out in your name and work to your glory.
> Grant us that grace that you gave to your disciples:
> come and raise us where we are.
> Amen.

Follow me!

————◆————

John 21.7–25

Risen Jesus, help me take a leap of faith for you
and plunge into the waters of life,
eager to meet you, ready to live for you.

Let's pick up where we left off yesterday, by the shore of Galilee. The breakfast is over, the men no longer hungry, and the fire's burning more gently now. It all sounds quite homely, but there's an awkwardness still between the friends and the risen Jesus. They aren't quite at ease, and no one is less at ease than Peter. There's unfinished business between himself and his master. Like a child that has to own up to Dad, or tell a close friend 'I'm sorry, I messed up', there's a barrier between them that won't be lifted till he 'comes clean'. Until he finds the right words, Peter's relationship with Jesus will remain marred by that dreadful threefold denial of him during the trial.

But Jesus looks at it differently, and so can we. What was it Peter did when he first realized the stranger was the Lord? He jumped into the water, rushing to meet him. The character of impetuous Peter leaps off the page just as he leapt out of the boat and plunged into the sea – a baptism by total immersion through which Peter's sins were washed away, and Jesus didn't have to rebuke him or even insist that Peter spoke the words. Before the resurrection, Jesus had had the power to heal the sick and turn water into wine, to still the storm and drive out demons, but he'd never been allowed to change Peter. But now, Peter's born again, as through baptism.

Jesus, help me acknowledge the moments when
I seal up my self from your rescue,
and refuse your offer to change.

Peter gained wisdom the hard way, through failure and disgrace. Whether so emotional a man as Peter actually thought this through reflectively, we can't be sure, but at the deepest level, in his heart, he was restored. At our baptism we are asked, 'Do you turn to Christ, do you repent of your sins; do you renounce evil?' Now Jesus posed three questions to Peter, questions which carry the same meaning. 'Simon son of John, do you love me more than these?'

> Lord, you know that my love is feeble;
> help my love become stronger
> in response to the love you offer me.

Jesus went through the deep waters of death in order to bless, wash, cleanse and raise us, and that is what he did for Peter. He received him back into fellowship, and the hurt was healed and the man redeemed. This moment approaches the holiness of a sacrament.

The 'baptism' of Peter isn't just for Peter's sake, however, just as our baptism isn't just for us. We are called to 'shine as a light in the world to the glory of God'. Peter was given not just forgiveness, but responsibility. He was called upon to care for and feed the flock. And then came the ultimate command: 'Follow me!'

Peter finally realized that Jesus, as the fullest expression of God's love, was still actively alongside him, enabling him to go forward transformed. After Peter was cleansed of his sins he has access to the same, complete, reconciled relationship with Jesus that Jesus had with God the Father. And that is the point of the resurrection for us all.

> Lord, in my heart, I renew my baptism vows.
> Marked now with the sign of your cross,
> lead me into a transformed relationship with you.
> Amen.

Brothers reunited: Jacob and Esau; Joseph and his brothers

Genesis 32—33, 42—45

> Risen Jesus, shine your resurrection light into
> the darkness of lives
> burdened by sin and overtaken by tragedy.

It may be surprising in Easter week to turn back to the Old Testament. During Lent, we visited some stories which featured a vicious circle of destructive behaviour, particularly in Genesis. But even before the incarnation of God's son, glimmers of reconciliation and hope can be found, presaging the resurrection.

When we greet someone at the airport or the station or the front door, whom we haven't seen for ages, it is usually with beaming faces.

> Welcoming God, help us greet the other with joy,
> and embrace them with acceptance.

Not so in the reunion of Jacob and Esau. When we last met Jacob (Week 3), he was in exile and Esau was in despair after his brother's double betrayal. First Jacob had tempted away his birthright, and then, more dreadfully, tricked him of the blessing due the firstborn son. Jacob laboured long and hard in exile and met many challenges and unkindnesses, until he heard God's word telling him to return to his homeland. But dared he risk the wrath of Esau? He prepared his return with as much stealth and intrigue as we've come to expect from this clever operator, and we are never absolutely convinced by his display of regret. He seemed to humble himself to Esau at the same time as preparing a retreat.

But Esau's response was without duplicity or doubt. 'Esau ran to meet Jacob and embraced him; he threw his arms around his neck and kissed him. And they wept' (Genesis 33.4). How like the father in Luke's story of the lost son this sounds! His was a noble character, totally without guile, who had resisted bitterness and kept his heart open and able to forgive. It didn't seem to matter to Esau whether his brother was genuine or not; the reunion was its own reward. Esau's generous spirit set Jacob free to become the full person God intended.

> Risen Jesus, may we learn to overcome hurt and injury,
> and be big-hearted enough to forgive.

In another Genesis reconciliation, that of Joseph and his brothers, we see real repentance and true forgiveness. The brothers had been so jealous of the young brother, who was their father Jacob's favourite son, that they'd plotted his murder, and only through chance events was his life spared. Though he was sold into slavery in Egypt, his adventures continued and led to him rising to become Pharaoh's right-hand man. When the guilty brothers arrived years later in Egypt to buy food during the famine, they didn't recognize Joseph at all, but through a series of tests, they began to reflect and they remembered their sins of envy, malice and violence. 'Surely we are being punished because of our brother . . . when he pleaded with us for his life, but we would not listen,' they said (Genesis 42.21). This insight made them realize they were now in the position they had condemned their brother to so many years before.

Joseph tested them a second time, demanding that Benjamin, his full brother, and the comfort of Jacob's old age, be brought to him. Benjamin was arrested for a theft he did not commit, and when Judah made the great connection: 'God has uncovered your servants' guilt', he offered to sacrifice himself for Benjamin's release. Joseph was at last certain that they had learnt wisdom and love. More importantly, they had learnt empathy and altruism, the ability to identify with the other, and imagine their father's pain, and put the protection of another before their own safety. Joseph's revelation that he was alive must have seemed like a miraculous resurrection to the brothers, but the true resurrection took place in their hearts.

In these two ancient stories we see exile and return, sin and repentance, rivalry and reconciliation. They prove that the pattern of exclusion and destruction can be transformed.

Risen Jesus, rise in my heart today,
transform my perception through your Spirit,
bring meaning, and value, and the searchlight of conscience
to all my relationships.
Amen.

I am the living bread:
Elijah and the widow of Zarephath

---•◆•---

1 Kings 17; John 6

My Father . . . gives you the true bread. . . .
that comes down from heaven and gives life to the world.
(John 6.32–33)

If we only have bread and water, life is possible, whatever adversity we endure; without it, no amount of luxury will keep us alive. In the time of Elijah, the people of Israel got their priorities wrong and excluded God from their lives and society, so the prophet declared 'there will be neither dew nor rain in the next few years except at my word' (I Kings 17.1). We are in yet another wilderness story, where hunger and thirst threaten existence. The people experienced God's withdrawal, vividly expressed by Elijah being sent by God to a foreign neighbourhood. There Elijah had to struggle for the basics of life. Ravens brought him food and a small brook gave just enough water, until even that ceased to flow. So the wilderness threatened to overpower even Elijah.

But then God sent Elijah to find a woman – a widow, so poor that when we meet her she is gathering sticks, and a foreigner – an outsider, a pagan. The widow of Zarephath had all the characteristics of the people Jesus sought out, too: she ticked all his boxes! 'Would you bring me a little water in a jar so I may have a drink?' Elijah asked her. And while you're at it, 'please, a piece of bread'. This is the man who has prophesied the famine, and yet he's the one asking for help. He'd eat her out of house and home; he demanded of her everything. Her reply was to explain she was preparing the final meal for her son 'that we may eat it – and die' (v. 12).

Why would this woman have been so compliant? Surely it's no coincidence that she was a woman. This may be because they are more attuned to the suffering and joy of creation, living the cycle of death and resurrection in their bodies as they do. It may also be because they were the 'poor in spirit', practically and personally powerless. Women like this widow were the last in the pecking order, and so they became the first in the kingdom.

> I am the bread of life.
> She who comes to me will never be hungry
> And she who believes will never be thirsty.
> (cf. John 6.35)

God finally acted. 'The jar of flour will not be used up and the jug of oil will not run dry until the day the LORD sends rain on the land,' Elijah declared. It sounds just like the children's story of the everlasting porridge pot! But just as the widow's life began to improve, it got worse again. Her larder was replenished but the son grew sick. How often we meet people who struggle out of one adversity only to be stricken by another blow, like the neighbour who recovers from a long illness, only for his wife to be made redundant. And so the worst happened in this story too: the son died, and the woman cried out against Elijah and his God. The pattern of wilderness and death seemed set to continue. But this is not the story's end, for here, deep in the pages of the Old Testament, we find the first raising from the dead, as Elijah stretched himself out on the lifeless body of the son and gave him the kiss of life, praying 'Let this boy's life return to him!' (1 Kings 17.21).

> I am the living bread . . .
> Whoever eats this bread
> will live for ever. (John 6.51)

For us, the revival of hope, the resurrection moment, may not always be so dramatic. It may just be a 'breath of fresh air' – but one like that 'breath of fresh air' referred to in Stevie Smith's poem, 'Black March' (*Emergency Kit*, p. 113). Without fresh air, we die.

The experience will be a turning point, one we carry always in our memory as the time we finally put a burden down or our way became clear, and life compelled us to begin again.

There have been many echoes of Jesus' stories and teaching in this story of the widow of Zarephath. Though of course, echo is not the right word, for an echo is a fainter version of an earlier sound, a weaker repetition. But in this case, it is the reverse: the story of the widow's encounter with Elijah is the earlier, muted version, and the life and death and resurrection of Jesus is the crescendo.

> This bread is my flesh,
> which I will give for the life of the world.
> Amen.   (John 6.51)

Listen to everything:
Philip and the Ethiopian;
Peter and Cornelius

Acts 8, 10

Risen Jesus, help us listen well to those who accompany us
in life,
whose view is further down the road we are called to travel.

Two stories in Acts are marvellous examples of new life, and new life
brought about through the mediation of another. Not only that, but
they show how, after Pentecost, the disciples, having grown Christlike
themselves, became able to change people as once Jesus had done,
through deepening relationships.

In the mysterious story of the disciple Philip and the Ethiopian
(Acts 8), Philip was alerted by an angel to seek out an Ethiopian
travelling along the road from Jerusalem to Gaza; and as he went
along, the Ethiopian was immersed in reading Isaiah. Maybe he was
a Jewish convert, or at least very interested. The foreigner was scratch-
ing his head over his Bible study, and Philip helped him understand
the 'good news', almost in the same way that Jesus had with the disciples on the road to Emmaus. The Ethiopian was so convinced, that
then and there he was baptized. At this point, Philip disappeared, his
work done. The new convert had to continue his journey alone, but
now forever changed, and starting afresh.

Lord, you sent Philip out into the desert
to bring a stranger into your kingdom.
Give me the knowledge to help another
meet you in your word.

142

A few chapters later, we find a similar pattern, when Peter's help is requested by Cornelius, a centurion of the Italian Regiment. Here we meet another outsider, but one who was already attracted to the ethics and God of the Jews, and keen to learn more. Through the intervention of another angel, Cornelius sent for Peter. It seemed he had no reluctance to accept Peter's wisdom, despite the gulf in their race and status, for when Peter, the former fisherman, arrived at the Roman's house, the centurion 'fell at his feet in reverence'. But Peter hastily insisted, 'I am only a man myself.' He affirmed their common humanity, despite the many differences between them.

> Your wisdom can be spoken by the simple;
> may I never be too proud to hear it.

Like Philip and the Ethiopian, this encounter with Peter led to Cornelius's baptism. There are times when intermediaries will be important in all our lives. Cornelius needed an angel to tell him about Peter, and Peter needed the messengers to fetch him, and the Holy Spirit needed Peter before the Spirit could descend 'on all who heard the message'. To meet God through the word, they had to meet God in another person first, and learn trust in God through trust in a relationship.

The story ends with Peter's wonderful declaration: 'I now realise how true it is that God does not show favouritism but accepts from every nation the one who fears him and does what is right.' And for nation, let us read class, gender and sect.

The story of Cornelius has another significance, because it is the confirmation of Peter's own extraordinary threefold vision in Acts 10.11–16, of the sheet filled with creatures, impure and unclean, which he was ordered to eat. As the food was strange, foreign and taboo, so were the Ethiopian and Cornelius strangers, and suspect. But Christ treated perfect strangers as if he'd known them all his life. He had compassion on people whose name he'd never known. And so the taboo between gentile and Jew was broken, and Peter and Cornelius were changed for ever. Both Philip and Peter took on Christ's powers to win strangers for Christ. They carried on the work of Jesus of healing this divided world.

143

Lord of all, you exclude no one from your loving purposes,
and your will is for every one of us to be made new.
Thank you for the people who have helped me to change,
and may I learn to be an evangelist, too.
Amen.

For three days he was blind: Paul

Acts 9

> Risen Christ, when I can't see properly, open my eyes.
> When I don't think clearly, straighten out my thoughts.
> When I won't act with love, soften my heart.

Just think how amazing the eye is, and how extraordinary a thing sight is. I remember being fascinated by the biology lessons that taught me the complexities of cornea, iris, pupil and lens. Do you know that there actually is such a thing as a 'blind spot'? Then I learnt, more amazing still, of the refraction of rays of light, the inverted picture at the back of the eye, the nerve fibres that carry the messages, and the brain which finally prints the picture the right way up! For it is the brain that does the seeing; it is only once the light reaches the brain that the proper meaning is interpreted in our consciousness, and reality revealed.

> I thank you for the extraordinary beauty of your world
> and pray for the blind and partially sighted,
> that they may experience your riches in other ways.

Saul saw everything upside down, too. He couldn't see past his blind spot – his hatred, fear and persecution of the followers of 'the Way'. So he set out on a journey from Jerusalem to Damascus, 'still breathing out murderous threats against the Lord's disciples' (Acts 9.1). No travel in those days was risk free, but he had almost arrived without incident before his whole world came crashing down. In a flash he was blinded – for three days. He had to be led along the road called 'Straight Street' to sanctuary. It was his new Lord Jesus who had preached 'strait *is* the gate, and narrow *is* the way' which leads to life (Matthew 7.14, KJV), and Paul's steps actually traced this truth.

In those three days, while ministered to by a reluctant but obedient disciple, Ananias, he was transformed – healed, restored and forgiven. 'Something like scales fell from Saul's eyes, and he could see again' (Acts 9.18). Three days in which a total reversal of his beliefs and attitudes took place; three days for a new man to arise, to experience his own 'resurrection'. He had been led to the house by hand – like a little child. When he left the house, he was a grown man again, walking only with the hand of Jesus. Paul had all the strength and talent he had needed to be God's servant, but he had lived in the dark, and now he was in the light.

> Lord Jesus, give me the insight to see
> a situation or an experience
> in a different way, in a new light.

Paul didn't know what lay ahead; none of us do: 'Faith enlightens the path behind you but as a rule the front of you is still in darkness, but not so threatening' (R. Rohr, *The Naked Now*, p. 120).

Try counting how many times a day you use the word 'see'. And check in how many different ways you use it. Even many blind people will use the verb, not inhibited or reluctant because they know it means much more than just the making out of shapes and colour. It doesn't just mean to look, watch or observe. We use it automatically to mean we discern something mentally – we understand. We use it when we mean we consider something – 'let me see about that'. We use it to mean we've learnt something, or on reflection we'll wait until we know more. We use it to mean we are interpreting things – 'I see things differently now'. We use it to indicate our belief – 'as I see it'. In all these ways, Saul's sight was tested. The picture he'd clung to was reversed, the life he'd led was reversed – or rather, turned the right way up at last.

> Risen Jesus, God of light and sight,
> grant me a discerning heart.
> Illuminate my life, my mind and my vision,
> and make the scales fall from my eyes this Easter.
> Amen.

Appendix:
An alternative order for Holy Week

Palm Sunday	Week 6, Sunday	Your King comes to you
Maundy Thursday	Week 4, Saturday	The full extent of his love
	Week 5, Friday	Betrayed by a word, betrayed with a kiss: Judas and Jesus
Good Friday	Week 6, Thursday	I am innocent of this man's blood
	Week 6, Friday	Several excuses for not following Jesus to the cross
	Week 4, Friday	Mary at the foot of the cross
	Week 5, Saturday	In two minds: Joseph of Arimathea
Holy Saturday	Week 6, Saturday	The empty room

Sources and acknowledgements

————◆◆◆————

The publisher and author acknowledge with thanks permission to reproduce extracts from copyright material. Every effort has been made to seek permission to use such material in this book. The publisher apologizes for those cases where permission might not have been sought and, if notified, will formally seek permission at the earliest opportunity.

T. S. Eliot, *Murder in the Cathedral*, London: Faber and Faber, 1964. From *The Complete Poems and Plays* by T. S. Eliot, copyright © Faber and Faber Ltd. Reproduced by permission.

Philip Larkin, 'This be the verse', in *Collected Poems*, London: Faber and Faber, 2003. From *The Complete Poems* by Philip Larkin, copyright © Faber and Faber Ltd. Reproduced by permission.

Robert Llewelyn (compiler), *Enfolded in Love: Daily Readings with Julian of Norwich*, London: Darton, Longman and Todd, 1980.

Richard Rohr, *The Naked Now: Learning to See as the Mystics See*, New York: Crossroad, 2009.

Society of St Francis (compilers), *A Sense of the Divine: A Franciscan Reader for the Christian Year*, Norwich: Canterbury Press, 2001.

Stevie Smith, 'Black March', in *Emergency Kit: Poems for Strange Times*, ed. Jo Shapcott and Matthew Sweeney, London: Faber and Faber, 1996.

J. Neville Ward, *Friday Afternoon*, London: Epworth Press, 1976.

Keith Ward, *The Promise*, London: SPCK, 2010.

H. A. Williams, *True Wilderness*, London: Fontana, 1976.

Index of biblical stories and references

———◆———

Old Testament

New Testament